Daddy's Little Earner

Daddy's Little Earner

A heartbreaking true
story of a brave little girl's
escape from violence

MARIA LANDON

with Andrew Crofts

HarperElement
An Imprint of HarperCollins*Publishers*
77–85 Fulham Palace Road,
Hammersmith, London W6 8JB

and *HarperElement* are trademarks
of HarperCollins*Publishers* Ltd

First published by HarperElement 2008
This edition 2008

1

A catalogue record of this book is
available from the British Library

ISBN-13   978-0-00-726877-1
ISBN-10   0-00-726877-7

Printed and bound in Great Britain by
Clays Ltd, St Ives plc

To Glen
Love you and miss you always xx

'Pause you who read this, and think for a moment of the long chain of iron or gold, of thorns or flowers, that would never have bound you, but for the formation of the first link on one memorable day.'

Charles Dickens – *Great Expectations*

introduction

'Ria, you're my favourite,' Dad would tell me through-
out my childhood. 'All daddies love their little
girls the best.' I'd fill with pride at this announcement
from my big, handsome, heroic father. I was his special
one. My brother Terry might be Mum's favourite but Dad
loved me most and I'd have done anything to please him.

Mum says that right from the start he boasted to all
and sundry that he was going to train me to be 'the best
little prostitute on the block', but I only gradually got an
inkling of what that meant. I probably didn't want to
know so I blocked it, even when he brought home his
prostitute friends and dressed me up in their clothes.
Even when he started breaking me in.

Years later, when my testimony put him in jail for
living off my immoral earnings, he said: 'You can cut me
into a thousand pieces but I'll always put myself back

together again and I'll be there for you, no matter what you do. I'm the only one who will ever truly love you.'

I think he genuinely did love me, to the extent that he was capable of love, and I stayed a daddy's girl right into my teens. He was my dad, the only one I had, after all. And he had a lot of charm, he could talk the birds down from the trees. There are plenty of people, even now, who have a soft spot for him, despite knowing everything he's done.

Without that charm, none of it would ever have happened. Mum wouldn't have fallen head over heels for him, a lot of other people wouldn't have got hurt, and I wouldn't have found myself working the streets at the age of thirteen to keep him in booze.

Every little girl has the potential to be a pop star, a ballerina, a doctor, a barrister, a policewoman or a prostitute, but to make the right choices they need support and guidance from the people whose responsibility it is to care for them. With a dad like mine, I never stood a chance.

Daddy's Little Earner

Chapter One

a glamorous couple

Terry and Jane, my mum and dad, were always described as a glamorous couple. Anyone who knew them when they were young in the early 1960s would agree on that, however much they might later disapprove of the way they both behaved. It was obvious to everyone that they absolutely adored one another; you might even say they were obsessed, and that it was their obsession with one another that led to so many of our problems.

If they were both the loves of one another's lives, as they undoubtedly were, you would have thought that would have given us, their children, a secure start in life – but there were other darker elements of their relationship at work almost from the moment they met, which turned our family and our lives into a nightmare.

Everyone in the pubs that he frequented loved Dad. He was tall and handsome, with dark hair and a powerful presence about him. He was invariably immaculately dressed in a suit and tie and known for being good company wherever he was, never able to resist playing up to an adoring crowd of admirers.

Mum was only five feet four, but she had a perfect figure, slim but curvy, which she readily showed off with mini skirts, hot pants and tightly fitted tops, everything that was fashionable amongst the young in those days, even in Norwich, a good few miles away from 'swinging London'. I don't have any early memories of her but I'm told she was strikingly beautiful, with long jet-black hair, deep brown eyes and flawless skin.

Dad was the black sheep of his family, or so the legend was whispered, the one with a dubious past who never did the right things but who prided himself on doing the wrong things with style. He always claimed that he was conceived when his mother had a fling with another man during the war, while his father (his mother's husband, that is) was away from home doing the honourable thing and fighting for king and country. If that was true it would certainly go some of the way towards explaining why Dad was so different to the rest of his family, and why we were always treated as though we were outsiders in some way that was never actually put into words. Having a different father to his siblings meant there was always a gap between them and him. His life seemed to travel on totally different tracks to theirs, partly from his own choice and partly because of the way he was and the things he believed. Maybe the fact that he had a different father was also the reason why Dad was his mother's favourite, the one she would always stick up for no matter what he did.

Her husband, who was a farmer, got into a lot of debt when he came back from the war and, unable to see a way out, he shot himself in the shed at the bottom of their garden. Dad said he was the one who found the body when he was still just a small boy. No one else ever verified that story for me so I have no way of knowing if it was true, but I certainly believed it at the time. Maybe it was true. Whatever happened, I certainly didn't have a grandfather on that side and Nanny lived alone in her bungalow a few miles away from us.

Rumour also had it in the family that my dad and my grandmother slept in the same bed until he was fourteen. That seems very believable, given how close they were and how she tried to protect him from everyone, including me. It might also have explained why he was as relaxed as he was about everything to do with sex and nudity.

My aunts and uncles all grew up to be very different to Dad, quite middle class in their values and successful in their lives. They've bought their own homes and run their own businesses and none of them would have wanted to have anything to do with the sort of people that Dad liked to hang out with, the thieves, alcoholics and prostitutes who trooped in and out of our home at all hours of the day and night, and drank with him in the pubs of Norwich.

Dad didn't learn to read and write until long after I could – and I know he spent some time in an approved school as a boy, although no one ever told me what for. There was a story about him throwing a bus driver off the bus when he was still quite young and I believe the chap later died of a heart attack, although I don't know any more details. I doubt anyone could have been sure the two events were directly linked but it sounds like the sort of thing Dad might have done. As well as being a charmer he was also a bully and a show-off and he had an uncontrollable temper, which he frequently vented with violence.

Although Mum's family lived in a council house and hadn't done as well as some of Dad's relatives, she had been a bit spoiled by her father. Like Dad, she was always a problem to her parents in her early teens, running away from home, being wild and causing them no end of worry. Mind you, she can't have been that wild because on the night she met Dad, when she was still fifteen, she had gone out to the pictures on a date with another lad and when he tried to put his hand up her skirt in the dark she was mortified and slapped it away. Apparently affronted by such forward behaviour she immediately ran out of the cinema and set out to walk home alone, having successfully protected her honour. Just up the road she bumped into Dad, whom she had never met before. He was only a couple of years older than her but was already very skilled at laying on the charm and flattery. He was tall and well-dressed, a proper ladies' man, and her head was turned. He must have worked some magic because he didn't meet with any of the resistance the poor guy in the cinema had encountered and they ended up having sex together that very first night. That was how the great love affair, which was to destroy so many lives, began.

When Dad first brought Mum home, my grand-mother was overjoyed and immediately encouraged them to get married and start having children, but of course they had to wait until Mum was old enough. Dad had been in a fair bit of trouble when he was younger, always drinking and mixing with the wrong crowd, and Nanny was probably relieved to think she could get him off her hands, hoping he would settle down now that he had met the right woman.

Mum's parents were not as pleased by this great love match as Dad's mum was. In fact they went to court to try to stop her from seeing him. As she was only fifteen I sup-pose they thought they had a chance of saving her from him before it was too late. They must have been able to see through his charm and bravado immediately and they despised him, believing he was no good and would end up hurting their daughter. As it turned out they were completely justified in their fears. They had probably hoped she would meet some steady guy with a regular job who would be able to calm her down, and anyone meeting Dad would have known instantly that he was not going to be the man for that job.

The more her parents told her not to see him, of course, the more determined she became. By disapproving of her choice her parents had turned the affair into something illicit, adding to its glamour and excitement, making Dad seem like a forbidden fruit. From the first moment they spoke up against him they didn't stand a chance of keeping two such wilful, self-destructive kids apart.

Mum was nineteen when she fell pregnant for the first time, and they got married a week or two after my brother Terry Junior was born in 1965. Dad's mum was thrilled; I think she paid for the marriage licence and everything. Mum's parents must have realized they had lost the battle by that stage and were going to have to make the best of a bad job. Perhaps they hoped that having a baby would make Terry and Jane settle down a bit and take their responsibilities seriously.

I was born a year later, in 1966, followed three years after that by Christian and then by Glen in 1970. Right from the word go I was a proper little daddy's girl. I adored him, while Terry was more of a favourite for Mum.

'The moment you were born you were his,' Mum once told me, and I knew it was true. He loved my brother Terry too, but once I was born Terry became Mum's and I was his. The night of my birth I'm told he paraded around the hospital, completely drunk and smoking a cigar, much to the annoyance of the sister in charge.

'Right from the start,' Mum said, 'from when you were born, he used to joke that he was going to make you the best little prostitute on the block.'

Chapter Two

early home life

Beneath the glamorous act that Mum and Dad put on for the world when they were out around the pubs, things must have been pretty grim for them. While Terry was a baby they lived in a bed-sitting room, and it was only after I was born that they were given their own council house. If Dad had a job in those days it would have been painting and decorating, but I never knew him to do much work when he was a grown man and I can't imagine he was any different in his early twenties. He always says he worked in the early days when he and Mum were together, but she would say he didn't do much.

As a some-time decorator, Dad was able to do the house up a bit himself, but he only bothered with the parts that he saw and wanted to show off to the people he brought home at night. Their bedroom was beautiful and so was the sitting room, but the kitchen and outside toilet were horrible and our rooms were all bare boards and disgusting old wallpapers left by previous occupants; we had no curtains or furniture or light bulbs. We were given a couple of blankets each and there was no heating. I used to get myself dressed under the blankets in the morning, unable to face stepping out into the freezing room until I had on as many layers as possible.

Mum was very glamorous in those days, good at making the most of herself with make-up and clothes, and she owned an array of wigs to change her look when she wanted to. She used to sing around the pubs and clubs she and Dad frequented and she was keen to do more with her talent, maybe even going professional. She had a terrific, soulful voice and got a chance to appear on *Opportunity Knocks*, which was like the *X-Factor* of the time, but Dad wouldn't let her do it. I guess he was frightened he would lose control of her if she became successful, that he would be out of his depth amongst the sort of people she would meet and that she would leave him behind. Perhaps he was frightened she might meet someone else, someone who would treat her decently. It's quite likely that the audition would have come to nothing, but then again it could have been her chance to get out of her life with him, make some money and get some independence, and he wasn't about to let her do that. Everyone, even people who seem to have drawn all the short straws in life, gets a few chances to make something of their lives. If enough of those chances are missed, the options begin to shrink.

Not that the two of them weren't enjoying themselves for a lot of the time in the early days of their marriage, despite their money problems and Dad's violent temper. They both liked going out drinking together and Terry and I would be left at home or would have to sit outside the pubs with Cokes and crisps and wait for them to roll back out. Sometimes we would be sitting there for hours on end before they finally emerged, weaving around and slurring their words. I'm told that when I was about three they came out of The Lamb in Norwich and found I'd gone from wherever they had told me to sit. Suddenly frantic for their lost child, they got the police involved and they found me at the bus station with a woman who was about to board a bus with me. I wonder sometimes what would have happened to me if the police had got there a few minutes later. Could my life with this stranger have been any worse than it was soon to become anyway? I'll never know.

They were already developing a habit of spending every penny they had on drink. I'm pretty sure Dad wasn't working at that time because Mum's parents used to come round to our house every week with groceries and Mum had been in trouble with the law for breaking into the electric meters and things like that; so money must always have been pretty tight.

Apart from regularly announcing that he was going to make me a prostitute as soon as he could, Dad made plenty of other declarations that showed how little he took his role as my father seriously. Mum told me that when I was three he asked her to go down to the bookies to put a bet on for him. She didn't leap up immediately and he grew impatient. Dad liked to get instant obedience from all of us. Grabbing hold of me he pulled my dress up and yanked my knickers down.

'If you don't hurry up,' he shouted at her, 'I'm going to have her by the time you get back.'

I guess he was joking, but not many fathers would make any sort of joke about raping their three-year-old daughter and it was just one more comment that sowed a seed of concern in Mum's mind. She could never be sure what he was capable of or where he would draw the line of acceptable behaviour. Dad saw life differently to most decent people.

Occasionally Dad would come into a lump sum of money, mainly when he'd had a win on the horses, but also later when he bullied Mum into going on the game, and then he would really flash it around. No one could ever have accused him of being mean – quite the opposite. Even though he couldn't drive he bought himself a Mark 10 Jaguar one time and hired a friend called Eric to be our chauffeur. He took particular pleasure in being driven to the dole office to sign on each week, smartly suited and smoking a big cigar, thinking he was the cleverest man in the world because he was getting the better of the system. I don't know how he got away with it except that he was always so plausible people tended to believe whatever he told them.

His friends in the pubs loved him for these sorts of shows of bravado, and so did I. To me he was a hero. I remember sometimes when he was in the money he would actually light his cigars from the fire with ten or twenty pound notes. I thought that was the most brilliant thing imaginable, to have a father who was actually willing to burn money. How many little girls like me ever got to see such a shockingly extravagant sight?

Dad kept ferrets and he liked to put them into the inside pocket of his suit jacket when he went out to drink. It was like his little party piece in the pub to get them out and make all the women scream.

'Oh, Terry, Terry! You are a one!'

They all thought he was such a card. He always managed to collect a little mob of admirers around him wherever he drank; he was a born crowd puller.

Whether they had money or not Dad was always immaculately turned out with smart suits and ties and a clean shirt every day, even though he only ever went drinking in scruffy city pubs or into the bookies, never to anywhere where he needed to be dressed up. He would polish his shoes every night till he could see his face in them, wash his hair and shave every morning, preparing to put on another show for his public.

When he had cash he was always happy to spend it on things for the family, as long as they were things that would impress other people as well. We were the first people in our road to have a colour television and an automatic washing machine, for instance. Despite these flamboyant displays during the boom times, most of the time, of course, we didn't even have any food in the house or a change of clothes for either Terry or me. There was actually no spare money at all.

Dad loved his dogs and mostly had corgis, just to be unusual I think and because it meant he could boast that he had the same dogs as the Queen. Her Majesty is the only other person I've ever heard of who likes the breed so Dad could be fairly sure he wouldn't bump into anyone else with one down the pub. When I was little we had a standard poodle called Gina and a St Bernard, both far too big for our house but perfect props for Dad as he swaggered around town or welcomed friends into his little kingdom to drink, play cards and whatever else they got up to.

When he was a teenager, Dad's nickname had been Pussy because he used to wear a long pointed pair of winkle-picker boots and everyone started calling him 'Puss in Boots', so he called the first corgi Pussy too, making it an extension of his own ego. That dog used to follow him everywhere he went in the city, waddling along on its short little legs, panting eagerly, never wearing a collar or lead. Dad would have loved the idea that the dog was so fond of him and so well controlled it would never wander off; having it on a lead would have created completely the wrong image for him. Whenever Dad ended a day out by getting arrested for being drunk or for causing a fight, which was quite often, Pussy the corgi would be sent home on his own in a police car or a taxi. Everyone knew who he belonged to and it all added to the image Dad cultivated for himself of being a lovable local rogue and 'a bit of a character'.

Even when he had no money to feed or clothe his children, Dad thought it was perfectly normal for a man to go out drinking from the moment the pubs opened at ten thirty in the morning. As far as he was concerned it was his right to do whatever he wanted in life and he wouldn't tolerate anyone telling him any different.

One of the rights he insisted on was to do as he pleased with his children, and part of this meant beating us whenever the urge took him. We were as much his property as Pussy the corgi or his well-shone boots. We trotted eagerly around behind him on our short little legs just like the dog, desperate to please him and avoid punishments.

Maybe it was the help they got from their parents that meant they were able to cope with looking after Terry and me when we were babies, or maybe it was just the energy and enthusiasm of youth that carried them through. But by the time my little brothers Christian and Glen came along Mum and Dad were no longer coping as parents. For some reason Dad just couldn't bear having them around. Chris annoyed him so much that once he crammed him into the washing machine and threatened to switch it on while Mum was screaming hysterically at him to let him out. Not surprisingly Chris was absolutely terrified of Dad, cringing and shaking like a puppy expecting a beating whenever Dad was around, and clinging on to Mum's skirts for protection.

Mum's solution was to keep Chris and Glen locked in their bedroom together whenever Dad was in the house. I hardly remember seeing them at all, even though I was four when Glen was born. Mum would bring them downstairs to feed and bath them when Dad was safely out of the way but the rest of the time they were locked up. Normal babies would shout and scream for attention but they didn't. It was probably fear that kept them so quiet, making it easier for our parents to gradually forget that their two youngest children existed at all. Chris wouldn't have wanted to cry out for fear of attracting Dad's wrath and Glen probably started by following his brother's example and then eventually didn't have the strength to cry anyway. I suppose they must have given up hope of anyone responding to their needs and just fallen into a hopeless, fatalistic silence.

Chris and Glen's silent room really frightened Terry and me. We hated the terrible smells that it emitted, of faeces and stale urine, and we didn't dare to open the door or go in on our own, never knowing if we went in there whether we would find them dead or alive. I can still remember those smells and I will never forget the squalor of the room on the few occasions when I did go in there with a grown-up, but I don't remember ever hearing either of them cry.

I wish I could have done something to help them but I was only tiny myself. Besides, by this stage everyone in the house knew better than to defy Dad and risk his temper igniting. I was desperate to please him and to be in his good books, but more and more I seemed to get things wrong. One day when I was about four, we had been playing Ludo as a family and I must have got overexcited and rolled too violently, accidentally losing the dice.

'Find it immediately,' Dad ordered, his voice steely, but I just couldn't; however hard I searched through the carpet and under the furniture it remained stubbornly gone. Looking back now, I wonder if perhaps he secretly slipped it into his pocket to ensure that its discovery wouldn't spoil his fun. Once he had set his heart on beating one of us nothing was allowed to get in the way of his gratification.

Mum says he went out into the garden that day and cut a stick from a bush, choosing a particularly strong and bendy specimen. While the rest of us continued searching frantically for the dice he took a knife and methodically cut away all the leaves and twigs, leaving himself with a vicious-looking weapon which he swished through the air menacingly as if testing its suppleness. Mum knew what he was planning to do with it and pleaded with him not to but he took no notice. Dad never allowed anyone to talk him out of doing anything he had decided on.

When he was finally ready he ordered me to take down my knickers and laid me across his lap, holding me tightly and whipping me until I bled. I screamed with utter shock, completely devastated that my adored Dad could turn against me like this. The emotional betrayal was worse than the pain, although that was excruciating. I couldn't sit down for a week afterwards. That was the first time he ever beat me, but from then on the stick stayed on display in the sitting room, ready to be used whenever he lost his temper.

The blows themselves hurt badly enough, but it was the expectation of them that became the real torture. He would always tell us in advance that he was going to beat us, leaving the stick standing by the fireplace, just glancing at it now and again, reminding us what was coming, prolonging the dread and making me cry before he had even struck a single blow. He would tease us with it. 'Do you want some of this?' he would ask as he tested it against his own palm.

He didn't always use the stick – sometimes he would use a slipper – and he didn't need to be drunk in order to decide to grab hold of one of us, wrench down our pants and put us over his knee. Sometimes he was stone cold sober, feeling pissed off with life and wanting to take it out on someone smaller than himself.

'It's about time you had ten of these,' he would announce and we would know there was no getting out of it.

One day I remember in particular Dad issued one of his usual orders for me to go over to him to take a beating with his slipper. 'Take your knickers down,' he commanded and I was so frightened I stayed rooted to the spot and started to cry and plead with him even though I knew it was hopeless.

'Stop crying,' he ordered, 'or you'll get twenty hits instead of ten.'

The short walk across the sitting room towards him seemed impossible and I stayed rooted to the spot, out of his reach. I knew what would happen if I defied him but my legs just wouldn't move, like in a nightmare.

'Get here now!' he bellowed, furious at being disobeyed, and I jerked into life, lurching forward.

The nearer I got to him the more he smiled and for a split second I thought he had changed his mind, that he was just teasing me, having a bit of fun. Although my whole body was trembling with fear I forced my mouth to smile back at him, trying to make him love me enough not to want to hurt me. The moment I was within reach he grabbed me and threw me across his long legs. As he raised the slipper in the air I let out an almighty scream, which made him laugh.

'I haven't even touched you yet!'

I couldn't stop the crying and it made him angrier still so he doubled the number of hits to teach me a lesson, to teach me to be brave and strong, to teach me to obey his orders the moment they were issued. His lessons worked because I soon learnt to stifle my screams and take my punishments in silence. I always concentrated hard on counting each stroke to try to distract my mind from the pain and to keep myself from crying and angering him more.

Once he had finished he would throw me to the floor and I would scrabble to pull up my knickers, the tears silently streaking my cheeks, a wave of relief sweeping through me at the thought that it was over and that I had survived an ordeal that I had thought a few minutes earlier was going to kill me. Why had I made such a fuss? I would ask myself. It wasn't so bad. I was still alive even if my bottom did hurt. Maybe Dad was right and I was making a fuss about nothing. I would then crawl into a chair and try to sit down, but it would hurt too much and I would have to lean on my side. My punishment was over, but however hard I tried I wouldn't always be able to stop the tears. I would try to sniff them back up before he saw them.

'Stop snivelling,' he would bark, 'or you'll get another lot and this time it will be the stick!'

Him shouting would just make me want to cry more. I wanted to run over to him and tell him I was sorry for whatever I had done and that I still loved him. I wanted to ask him to hold me and cuddle me, but I knew better than to do that because such weakness would only aggravate him. So instead I would desperately fight to swallow my sobs and stop the tears from flowing.

I remember witnessing him beating up Terry really badly one day, punching him with his fists. I watched Terry sliding down the wall, the wallpaper behind him smeared with his blood. I couldn't intervene because I would have received the same treatment for daring to go against him, so I just had to watch and wait for it to be over. If you tried to ask why he was angry or to argue with him you would merely make the ordeal last longer and give him an excuse to become more vicious.

Mum was useless at protecting us because by this stage she was utterly terrified of him as well. He wasn't the kind of man that many people found the courage to resist. Gradually he undermined Mum's confidence, telling her she was ugly and useless. He used to beat her about as well, kicking her in the mouth once and knocking out some of her teeth so she had to get false ones. She still has a prominent scar on her chin from that attack.

Things must have been volatile between her and Dad

right from the moment they met but it was when she fell pregnant with Glen that she says it all started to go badly wrong. Dad was drinking a lot by then and when she was a few months pregnant they passed a Chinaman in the street on their way home from the pub. Maybe it started as a joke and then got out of hand, but Dad accused her of having an affair with him and then became convinced that Glen really was the Chinaman's baby. The whole idea was patently ridiculous since Mum had never set eyes on the man either before or after that chance passing in the street but Dad seemed to have convinced himself until he became so incensed by her imagined treachery that he threw Mum down the stairs with Glen inside her, sending her into premature labour. She had to have an emergency caesarean and, as they prepared her for the operation, the doctors discovered that she was suffering from anaemia and malnutrition. She was kept in hospital for a while receiving treatment for all her ailments.

Dad's theory about Glen having been fathered by a Chinaman was shown to be ridiculous once Glen was born because he looked more like Dad than any of us, but that didn't stop him from continuing with his delusion. He started claiming that he couldn't go out to work for fear that he would find Mum in bed with another man when he got back. I don't believe this for a moment, but he repeated it time and time again over the years to get sympathy, and I'm sure his cronies in the pub took him at his word. Poor old Terry, with a wife he couldn't trust.

When Mum was rushed into hospital for the caesarean, Terry Junior, Chris and I were placed with a foster family. I suppose Dad didn't think he could cope with us on his own or maybe Mum had told social services that he couldn't and that we needed to be protected from him. By that time I think the authorities were becoming aware of his violence. We must have been considered to be at risk.

One of the few memories I have of that period is of coming downstairs the first morning that I was in the foster home.

'Good morning,' one of the family said when they saw me appearing in the doorway and I froze, my face turning the colour of beetroot, totally unable to find the words to reply. The greeting must have taken me by surprise because people didn't exchange those sorts of simple pleasantries in our house; they just grunted and shouted at one another if they needed to communicate. From then on the foster family all called me 'dummy'. They may only have said it a few times, and they might just have been gently teasing me, but I was still mortified enough for the word to be burned indelibly into my memory. I knew it was my own fault for not speaking up as soon as I was spoken to, and it convinced me that I was inferior to the other children there, a worthless creature who had no right to be in their home at all but wasn't wanted by anyone else, least of all her parents.

When Mum had recovered from her operation we were allowed to go home again. The doctors said it could be dangerous for her to have another pregnancy and prescribed her with the contraceptive Pill. Once there was no danger of her falling pregnant again, Dad decided the time was ripe to put her on the game. He'd talked about it before, apparently, never seeing anything wrong with the idea. In fact it was a bit of a mystery to him why all women didn't do it.

'Every woman's sitting on a goldmine,' he would say. 'Pity I haven't had four girls because then I could run a proper little brothel and I'd never have to work again.'

It might seem ironic that he beat Mum up because he suspected she'd been unfaithful to him yet he was prepared for her to be a prostitute, sleeping with any man who could pay the going rate – but that would be entirely consistent with his warped kind of logic.

'If you're going to do it, you should get paid for it instead of giving it away for free,' he'd always say.

Chapter Three

putting mum on the game

Mum had never really taken him seriously in the early days of their relationship when he talked about her going on the game, assuming he was just joking. Who would imagine that any man would want to do that to the woman he loved? Why would he want to share her with any old Tom, Dick or Harry? But Dad wasn't like most men, and as the years passed Mum came to realize that. The comments that had started out sounding like a rather tasteless kind of banter between lovers grew to seem more real and threatening. And once she was on the Pill, Mum soon realized that he had become deadly serious with his plans and expected her to start excavating the 'goldmine' she was 'sitting on' and become the family breadwinner.

They probably already knew people who worked in the business because of the kind of places where they went to drink; Dad socialized with prostitutes all the time when I was a bit older. Selling your body simply didn't seem like a big deal to him; it was just another easy way to make good money for very little effort – well, very little effort by him.

It's hard to imagine how most men would have persuaded their wives to actually go out the first time and do it, but Dad had a way of making people do what he wanted with a mixture of charm, violent bullying and manipulation. Although he worshipped Mum, he constantly strove to control her in every way possible. He dominated and terrorized her almost as completely as he dominated and terrorized his children. When he wanted something, he would go on and on, like a terrier with a bone, never stopping until he got his own way, and I imagine that's how it was back then. He probably flattered her, telling her how gorgeous she was, then told her she was useless and how much she needed him, then he would nag her constantly that her family needed her to earn money, that it wasn't a lot to ask after all. I can imagine him doing it, and although it might be hard for other people to understand I know just how persuasive he could be when he set his mind to something.

And so Mum agreed. She says she allowed him to kid her that she was only going to have to do it once or twice, that he was just asking her to do him a favour because he was skint and this was the only way he could think of to make a bit of drinking money for them both quickly. The first time, he took her up to the block in Norwich where all the streetwalkers worked and explained to her what to say to the drivers of the cars that crawled along the kerbs and what to do once she was in the cars with them. I know exactly how he would have done that because a few years later he was making the same trip with me.

It wasn't long before Mum realized how naïve she was being. Easy money is as addictive as any drug, particularly if you don't have to do anything for it yourself. Once the cash started rolling in he was hardly going to put a stop to it; he probably wasn't capable of it, any more than he was capable of giving up his drinking or his gambling. The more she earned for him the more he wanted and the harder he made her work.

Dad took his role as a pimp very seriously, hanging around the block all night at first, making sure Mum stayed on her patch and took advantage of every single potential client who drew up. He would never allow her to go home until he felt she had extracted every penny possible from the punters. Whenever she had an unsavoury or threatening client and became frightened she would plead with Dad to let her stop but he ignored her, pretending he couldn't hear her and pushing her back to the edge of the street.

Mostly she would be getting into the men's cars at the kerb, driving off and transacting the business in the passenger seats, but sometimes she would bring the customers back to our house. Dad didn't mind how she did it as long as she kept working. He would sit downstairs watching the television while she was at work in their bedroom above, next to where Terry and I were sleeping and where Chris and Glen lay in silence. She would just have walked in the front door with the customer and gone straight up the stairs to do the business as if it was the most normal thing in the world. Dad saw nothing wrong with it at all.

She put up with it for two or three years, from soon after Glen's birth, all the while kidding herself that it would stop one day. Many years later she told me that she used to get so depressed she would sit downstairs all day reading books and eating chips until it was time to go out to work. For part of those years she had a day job at a shoe factory, so she must have been utterly worn out. She was struggling for her own survival and not able to take any notice of Terry or me and she seemed to forget all about Chris and Glen locked in their bedroom upstairs. Gradually, she brought them out of their room less and less, even when Dad wasn't there, until eventually she managed to forget they existed for hours on end. Maybe it felt as though she had too many things to cope with and something had to be allowed to give or her brain would have overloaded.

It's obvious from reading the social services records at the time how hard life must have been for Mum with four small kids and no money coming in apart from whatever she could keep back from Dad. It wouldn't have occurred to Dad to help her look after us either. I suppose there were a lot of men like that in those days. I don't think it would even have occurred to her to ask him for help because looking after the kids was considered to be women's work. But most husbands would have made sure they provided at least enough money for the basic essentials their family needed. If a traditional woman's place was at home looking after the house and the children, a traditional man's place was as the breadwinner for the family. Even when she was working Mum never got to keep anything she earned; it all had to be given to him to take down to the pub and the bookies. She was often forced to go to the authorities for help when there was no food in the house, but if he found out about it Dad would take whatever money they had handed out to her and would spend that on drink too. Sometimes the social services would give her vouchers and money for the electricity meter but then Dad would sell the vouchers and break into the meter when he needed more cash for the pub.

In the end Mum was left to rely on handouts from kind neighbours and the big parcel of groceries her parents brought round every Wednesday. It's hard to understand why my grandfather and grandmother couldn't see what was going on and do more to help us. I think they were at their wits' end to know what to do. I'm sure they can't have realized how bad things were for Chris and Glen, though; Mum must had cleaned them up a bit when her parents were due.

Once he'd had a few drinks Dad's obsession with Mum would sink into pure cruelty. He would pace up and down the front room for hours on end yelling at her about how fat, ugly and useless she was, telling her that no one would ever love her except him. If you tell some-one those sorts of things often enough they soon start to believe them.

'You've brought shame on the family,' he would rant. 'I should never have married you, you're just council house rubbish.'

They were living in a council house themselves at the time, but because the rest of Dad's family had done bet-ter and all owned their own businesses and homes he somehow thought that meant he was superior to her. There was no point in her arguing with him unless she wanted a beating so she just had to sit there and take whatever he wanted to throw at her.

I think it must have been 1972 the first time Mum left him, when I was about five years old. She always had trouble getting all four of us out of the house at the same time so she just took Glen and Chris with her to a local refuge for battered wives. I can understand why she thought they were in more danger from him than Terry and I were: they were so much smaller and he seemed to have taken against them from birth.

The NSPCC and local social services got involved in the case and after listening to what she had to say they went to visit Dad. The report came back that he was on the verge of having a nervous breakdown. I dare say these days they would have come up with a more specific diagnosis, such as 'bipolar disorder', but back then they just talked about depression and nervous breakdowns. They promised her they would have him admitted to the local psychiatric hospital for a month. During that time Mum was told she would be able to apply for a restraining order stopping him from returning to the house and she would get custody of all of us. For a few fleeting moments she must have felt that she was finally getting some protection from him, and that it was all going to work out.

Dad was taken off from the house in an ambulance and two social workers stayed with Terry and me until Mum arrived back home with Chris and Glen. Once they could see we were all settled in, the social workers left and a few minutes later Mum received a phone call from Dad to say he had escaped from the ambulance on the way to the hospital and had gone to his mother's to steal some of her sleeping tablets, which he was now swallowing.

'I took my own tablets before leaving home,' he told her, and at that moment Mum spotted the empty pill bottle standing on the kitchen table. 'I'll be dead soon so I'm ringing to say goodbye.'

He also, however, told her exactly where he was, so as soon as she had put the phone down on him she called the emergency services, who rushed to find him and take him to the hospital to have his stomach pumped. When Mum got there the doctors told her that if the ambulance had been ten minutes later he would have been dead. He was on a life-support machine for three days and went on to develop pneumonia. There's no doubt that Dad had a genuine problem with depression, but it was always hard to tell if he really wanted to go through with the suicide attempts or if they were 'cries for help'.

While Mum was visiting Dad in the hospital a senior psychiatrist came to talk to her. He'd been listening to Dad and had been appalled by everything he'd found out about their life together.

'You're married to a very dangerous man,' he warned her. 'Your husband is schizophrenic and in desperate need of psychiatric help. Frankly, I'm amazed you've managed to stay married to him for as long as you have.'

He arranged for Dad to be moved to the psychiatric hospital and Mum agreed to go in the ambulance with him. She must have been feeling relieved that someone else was recognizing her problem and finally helping her and she must have been worried about Dad too.

However badly he had been treating her, he was still the love of her young life and the father of her children.

'How long can they keep me here?' Dad asked the ambulance driver.

'They can't keep you here at all,' he replied. 'You're going in voluntarily.'

When he arrived at his destination the doctors tried hard to sedate him but he just kept saying he wanted to leave and ordering Mum to call him a taxi. She tried to put up a fight, tried to persuade him that it was for his own good that he got treatment, but ultimately there was nothing she could do once he'd made up his mind. Eventually she gave in and they got a taxi home, where their lives soon descended back to their previous level of violence and abuse, with Mum back working on the block every night of the week.

Mum tried to leave again, not long afterwards, and once more she went to a refuge for battered women. She stayed away longer this time and social services took Terry and me off to live with a foster family, some lovely people called the Watsons. They had a swimming pool in the garden of their Suffolk home where they carefully taught us how to swim. Dad had very different ideas on how these things should be done: one time he had slung us into the sea off the pier at Great Yarmouth, telling us that that would teach us how to swim. 'Sink or swim!' he laughed. As we survived the experience I suppose he must have been right, or maybe it was the current that washed us back up onto the beach along with all the other flotsam and jetsam, but I remember how terrifying it was floundering around in the waves, swallowing great mouthfuls of salty water every time I went under, compared to all the gentle help and encouragement the Watsons gave us.

They were such a sweet couple, trying everything possible to make us feel welcome and part of their family. We went blackberry picking and Mrs Watson made homemade pies and jams with us, but whatever we did and however nice they were to us I felt like an intruder. I knew I wasn't their child and I felt I shouldn't be there. It was never possible to really relax. I did wonder what made the Watsons' own children so much better than us that they deserved a life like this. Why wasn't I as special to my parents as their daughter was to them? My memory isn't very clear on dates and ages but we must have been with them a while because they put us into the local school, which was very sweet, and the teacher there taught me how to write.

However wonderful life was with the Watsons, I still wanted to be back home with my dad because that was where I felt I belonged. I wasn't good enough to deserve to live in a nice home like the Watsons'. I remember one particular afternoon, lying beside their swimming pool in glorious sunshine. Everything seemed so perfect. I had a beautiful new home and some new clothes they had bought for me. Mrs Watson brought us out cold drinks with ice cubes and fretted about me getting burned, rubbing sun cream onto my skin and making me feel so loved and cared for. But something wasn't quite right and I still felt sad. I wished I was someone else, a feeling I would grow very used to over the coming years.

Mum came with her parents a few times to visit us at that foster home. Although I have no memory of her I do remember my granddad being there. Mrs Watson was very understanding apparently and let Mum bath us and read us bedtime stories.

We were only allowed to see Dad for one hour a week during that time under supervision at the social services office. One week he didn't turn up and so they just took us back to the Watsons' in Suffolk. The following day he turned up at the social services office roaring drunk and highly agitated, demanding to see us, insisting that it was his right. The social worker, a Mr Ashby, explained to him that as we now lived so far away visits had to be arranged to suit everyone. Dad refused to see reason and started to beat the poor man up, having first locked the office door so he couldn't escape. The police eventually had to smash the door down and when they burst in they found Mr Ashby with three broken ribs, a broken nose, cuts and bruises. Dad was still on top of him, trying to gouge his eyes out when they finally dragged him off. That little outburst cost Dad a few months in prison but gave him something to boast about for years. He saw it as proof of how much he loved his kids, and how he wasn't willing to let some pen pusher come between us.

At the time Mum was convinced we would only be in foster care temporarily and that once she had got her act together she would have us back and would bring us up as a single mum. She assumed the authorities would be able to protect us all from Dad now they knew just how dangerous he could be. But once he was out of prison again Dad tracked Mum down and started to pester her to come back to him. He was always able to find her because of the involvement of social services in our lives. She moved and changed jobs twice to try to get away from him and both times he found her by insisting on his right to see his kids. Her employers and landlords would become tired of the harassment he would give her wherever she went and would ask her to leave.

Whenever Dad found her, he would just completely wear her down and promise things would be different and tell her he was the only one who loved her. Mum left him three or four times but each time he succeeded in making her go back to him again. And each time he would have her back out on the street again within a week.

By that time Mum had been arrested several times for soliciting and had a suspended sentence hanging over her, but Dad still forced her back to work. She was terrified of being picked up again and being sent to prison, but he wouldn't listen. One night she heard that the vice squad was doing a sweep of the area and she begged Dad to let her go home early since she had already earned plenty of money in the previous few hours. Dad wasn't willing to even consider it, becoming angry that she dared to suggest when she should stop work. It was his decision and not hers, as far as he was concerned. As they stood on the pavement beside the busy road he lifted her skirt up and started shouting at the passing cars.

'Come and get some of the best cunt in Norwich.'

Mum tells me that that was the final straw. At that moment she decided she was going to have to escape from him once and for all, whatever the cost, even if it meant abandoning her children to his mercies. She had run out of options. She had no choice any more.

Chapter Four

mum leaves

I have almost no memories of actually living with Mum although I was six when she finally left for good. I can't summon up any mental pictures of what it was like having her in the house with us. I have a vague memory of a woman making jellies at a birthday party but can't picture her face. There would be no children's parties after she left so it must have been Mum who was there in the kitchen making jelly. She says it was.

Nearly everything I have described so far I learned from her many years later or from other people who were around at the time, or from reading my social services records. It was always hard for Terry and me to piece together exactly what happened around the time she disappeared because Mum and Dad had such different views on it.

I do remember her coming back one time after one of her absences, although I still can't picture her face. To celebrate our reunion we all went to the pictures as a family, the four of us together. (I guess Chris and Glen were back at home in their room as usual.) I still can't actually visualize her being there, but I remember the event because as we came out of the cinema I got lost. I must have run on ahead in my excitement and taken a wrong turning. I don't think I was gone for that long, but when Dad found me he was really angry with me for inconveniencing him. When Mum finally left home he would tell me that I was the reason she had gone; that it was because I had got lost and been a nuisance to her that day after the cinema trip that she had decided she couldn't take any more. He was very good at making out everything that went wrong in his life was someone else's fault. I believed him because he was my dad so he must be right and because I already knew that I was a bad girl; he told me so all the time and had convinced me totally. So for years I believed it was all my fault that our mother had gone and that she no longer wanted to have anything to do with any of us.

I think each time Mum came back to Dad after one of her bids for freedom, she hoped that he would have been shocked into changing his ways, but each time he would start putting her down again, hitting her, nagging and bullying her to go back on the game again.

'Look,' he'd say, 'there's one of your punters. Why don't you do just one more?'

If she didn't respond to the cajoling then he would resort to violence. Nothing made him lose his temper more thoroughly than one of us refusing to do as we were told. Mum must have realized that as long as she was with him nothing was ever going to change, she was always going to have to do whatever he decided for her, that she would always be selling herself just to keep him in drinking and betting money. So she made up her mind to disappear once and for all.

One day in 1973 Mum sneaked home from the shoe factory in her lunch hour, when she knew Dad would be safely settled in the pub, and packed her case. Terry and I were probably sitting outside whichever pub Dad was drinking in. It didn't matter because she wasn't planning to take any of us with her this time. I suppose she knew that if she had children in tow Dad would be able to trace her through social services and make her go back to him. She wanted to vanish off the face of the earth. The psychiatrist's warnings about being married to 'a very dangerous man' must have been ringing in her ears as she hurried from the house for the last time with her few possessions hastily packed, slamming the door behind her. Chris and Glen would have been able to hear her movements from behind their bedroom door but by that stage they must have been so weak from hunger that they wouldn't have had the strength to cry out to her. There would have been no point anyway.

At first she went to a male friend and asked him to put her up. Initially he promised to care for her until she sorted herself out, but it wasn't long before she realized he was going to want to pimp for her just like Dad and she knew her only chance was to leave Norwich for ever and start afresh somewhere else, somewhere where no one knew about her past. When you're known to be a prostitute and all the people you socialize with belong to the same world, it's almost impossible to change anything as long as you stay in the same town; you have to make a clean break. Carrying the suitcase that contained all the possessions she had left in the world she walked out to the ring road on the edge of town and hitched a lift with a lorry driver.

'Where are you going?' she asked him.

'Blakeney,' he replied.

'That'll do,' she said and that was where she ended up. She was only about thirty miles up the Norfolk coast from us but as far as we were concerned back at home she might as well have been on the other side of the world.

She got herself a job in a hotel as a chambermaid and found a bed-sitting room. She contacted social services back in Norwich to tell them she'd gone and to ask them to take us into care, telling them yet again what her fears were for us. Her greatest fear, she said, was for me because of the number of times Dad had told her, and anyone else who would listen, that he was going to 'break me in' and put me on the game as soon as I was old enough. She knew him well enough to be sure that he wasn't bluffing. If he had been willing to put his own wife, the love of his life, on the game, why wouldn't he do the same to his daughter? She told them how dangerous she knew Dad was, feeling certain that they would take us away from him and put us into safe homes.

When the social workers arrived at the house that day, Dad was out with Terry and me but they must have broken in because they found Chris and Glen, who were two and three years old by then, abandoned in their locked bedroom as usual. Neither of them reacted to the strangers who suddenly appeared beside them. They just stared straight ahead with deadened eyes. Chris was rocking rhythmically back and forth in his cot and Glen was so hungry he was actually eating the contents of his own soiled nappy.

It was that scene, discovered by social workers, that sealed Mum's reputation as a terrible mother, giving Dad the opportunity to make out he was some sort of local hero by default. Even though the state those babies had got into was as much his fault as hers, he somehow managed to make himself seem like another victim of her neglect and cruelty rather than the cause of most of her problems. Mum says she was having a breakdown during her final years with us and I imagine that must have been what happened. There's no other explanation why a mother could neglect her own children to that extent.

I don't remember coming home that day to find Mum gone. Because she'd disappeared before, I probably assumed it was like the other times and she'd be back eventually. It was only gradually, over time, that I realized she wasn't coming back this time and that Terry, Dad and I were on our own now. I was six years old, nearly seven, and I had to become the woman of the house. A cold knot of panic formed in my chest when I thought about it.

The social workers took both Chris and Glen into care but, for some reason that no one has ever been able to explain to me, they decided it would be all right to leave Terry and me at home with Dad. Perhaps at that stage they thought Mum was the bigger problem; after all she was the one who was on the game, a lifestyle that carried so much stigma and suggested she couldn't possible be a decent parent, and she was the one who had deserted us. Perhaps they thought that with such a shameless woman gone from his life Dad might be able to do a better job for us. Who knows what he told them at the time to make himself look good and her look bad. Dad could convince anyone of almost anything when he put the full weight of his charm into it.

When Mum heard from her parents that Terry and I had been left with Dad she boarded the first train back to Norwich and went to see social services, to plead with them to do something. It must have been a nerve-racking trip for her, constantly looking over her shoulder for fear of being seen by someone who would tell Dad she was back in town. Both of the social workers she had dealt with in the past had been moved to other areas and she had to explain her whole story all over again to someone new. She pleaded and begged, telling them again about Dad's drinking problems, his violence, his involvement in prostitution and his promise that he intended to put me on the game as soon as possible. They refused to take her warnings seriously. Maybe they hear stories like that all the time and thought Mum was exaggerating to get back at her estranged husband.

'All your children are subject to care orders,' they tried to reassure her, 'which will stay in force until they are eighteen.' This was supposed to mean that social services took responsibility for us and made decisions about such things as where we lived and what schools we went to. No doubt they promised to keep an eye on us and to remove us if they thought we were in any danger, but I doubt if that would have put Mum's mind at rest. She knew how clever Dad was at manipulating people and making them believe whatever he wanted them to believe.

Although I have all my social services reports from the time, it is hard to work out from the things they have written why they made some of the decisions they did. I always felt hopeful in the following years whenever I knew that a social worker was due to call on us, because I thought each time they were bound to realize that something was wrong and would try to help us. But the main social worker who was allotted to us in the early years was so terrified of Dad she refused to come to the house unless she had a police escort or one of her bosses with her. Her visits were very infrequent and were over as quickly as everyone could manage. Her fears were not unreasonable, of course, since Dad had already served six months in jail for beating up that other social worker. But if they knew he was capable of that level of violence, did they not guess he was capable of being violent to us? What made them think it would be all right to give us straight back to him as soon as he finished his sentence?

Even if they had come visiting more often and asked us more probing questions it probably wouldn't have done them any good. I would never have spoken up to anyone in front of Dad, or even talked honestly about him if he weren't there. It would be years before I found the courage to do that. Sometimes I would sit silently staring at the social workers who did make it into the house, trying to talk to them with my mind, trying to send them messages, hoping they would be able to hear my telepathic cries for help, but of course they didn't. I have vivid memories of being asked questions like, 'Are you getting enough to eat?' and my stomach was rumbling but I didn't dare to say we hadn't had any food at all that day and only a few chips the day before. They took my silence as meaning that I had nothing I wanted to complain about. I would try to drop hints and clues but they never picked them up; maybe I was being too subtle or maybe they just didn't want to hear. It was bound to be easier for them if they could feel reassured that we were OK.

I was as terrified of Dad as anybody else, but I still adored him and wanted to be living with him. I just wanted them to make him be nice to us and to tell him to stop doing some of the things he was doing, such as beating us. I hated Mum for deserting us because I could see how devastated my brother and father both were and I despised her for abandoning them when they loved her so much. Hating her brought me even closer to Dad, giving us something else in common.

His broken heart was a terrible sight to behold, and I began to feel I had a responsibility to look after him. The worst times were always when he'd had a few drinks and the melodrama of his own self-invented life story would become heightened beyond anything any country and western songwriter would have dared to write. Time after time Terry and I would find him on the sitting room floor on his hands and knees, weeping and praying for 'his Jane' to come back to him, screaming hysterically at the gods in his abject misery.

He always became furious whenever Terry or I cried about anything, shouting at us to shut up, hitting us, seeing our tears as a sign of weakness, so I couldn't understand how he could be so willing for other people to see him cry so openly. For him it seemed to be like a badge of honour, a way to show everyone how wicked Mum was to have broken his heart and how much pain he was in.

'I can understand your mum leaving all the other children,' Dad would say to Terry, 'but not you because you were her favourite. How could she leave you? A mother is supposed to love her first-born child more than anyone.'

I would be able to see the pain in Terry's face as the words sank in, and feel my own pain at hearing someone confirm out loud that Mum had loved Terry more than me, even though I knew it to be true. Terry rarely cried but the tears would swell in his eyes at those moments and I was upset with Dad for being so cruel and for continually rubbing salt into my brother's emotional wounds.

However much I hated the way he behaved, Dad always managed to convince me of his undying love and favouritism towards me, as if to compensate me for the fact that my mother hadn't loved me enough to stay. He would assure me that as long as I stood by him everything would be OK.

'All mothers love their first sons and all daddies love their little girls,' he would say, as if merely saying it was enough to prove it was true. He never backed it up with displays of affection or kindness but these few crumbs were enough to keep my loyalty and adoration intact.

All the same, he managed to inflict maximum damage on both of us in his outpourings of misery. Terry would be heartbroken to think that his mother had done that to him and I would feel crushed to think that I hadn't been of importance to her, that only Terry would have mattered to her. Why would Mum have loved him more than me? I would wonder, deciding that it must be because I was such a bad person. Then I would decide not to care, telling myself that it didn't matter what she had felt for me because I was Dad's favourite and he was still there for us.

He had a particular skill at making other people feel so bad about themselves that they actually believed he was their hero, the only one who cared about them, the only one who was there for them when their lives fell to pieces. More often that not he would be responsible for reducing people to needy wrecks in the first place, then when he had them hooked and dependent on him he would remind them how useless they were, making them all the more grateful to him for being the one who looked after them. He did it with Mum and every other woman he ever went out with, and he did it to us children as well. I would go to him constantly, trying to climb onto his knee and telling him how much I loved him, but he would always push me away in disgust.

'You're too fat and ugly,' he was always telling me. 'No one will ever love you except me. Even your own mother left you.'

Looking back now I know I wasn't fat, just a normal healthy child, and I don't think I was ugly. But he convinced me of both at the time. Dad liked overweight women because they would be insecure about themselves and that would give him a chance to dominate and taunt them, calling them fat, useless whores.

Sometimes Dad would cuddle me, but it would only last a few seconds before he would shove me away again. I hated the feeling of rejection and eventually I stopped going to him. I still loved it when he told me I was his favourite, although it would make me feel sorry for Terry, but I didn't believe I deserved such an honour.

We weren't with Dad all the time because he quite often got taken off to prison for thieving or beating someone up. Whenever that happened Terry and I would be put back into foster homes and children's homes for a few months, or however long the sentence was. We were taken to visit him in prison sometimes and it was always a terrifying experience. Even sitting in the waiting room amongst the other visitors was intimidating. Everyone appeared to be so angry and aggressive and there always seemed to be the sounds of shouting in the distance, as well as the banging of the big iron doors and the clanking keys on the wardens' belts. It all added to the atmosphere of fear for small children who didn't understand half of what was going on or what was being said around them.

Once we were taken through to where he was waiting for us it was distressing to see our dad, who was normally so smartly turned out, reduced to baggy prison clothes, looking so vulnerable. We were used to him being the powerful one, the one in control of everyone around him, and it was unnerving to see him being forced into a sub-servient position, being bossed around by the wardens. He would become very emotional when he talked to us on those visits, promising that everything would be dif-ferent once he got home, that our lives would be wonder-ful and that he would get a job so he could buy us all the things we needed. It was as though he was playing some hard-done-by character from a country and western song – one man struggling bravely to bring his children up right in a hostile world. I always wanted to believe him, even when he kept on letting us down and breaking his promises, and I would always stick up for him in front of other people, even when I finally realized just how bad a father he really was.

As soon as he got out of jail, I would find a way to get back to Dad from wherever we were staying at the first possible opportunity. I felt I owed him my loyalty because, whatever he was like, at least he hadn't walked out on us like Mum had. He had stuck by us and so we belonged to him, we were his and it felt right that we should be with him. 'No one else will ever want you,' he'd say. 'Only me. You're fat and useless but at least you've got me.'

He couldn't stand the idea that Terry and I might be taken permanently into care because he didn't think it was anyone else's business how he brought us up, and because he didn't like to lose the benefits that he got as a single dad. We were his devoted little followers, part of his entourage, and he resented any attempts to part him from us.

He did try for many years to get Chris and Glen back as well, even though he had never known what to do with them when they were babies and wouldn't have been any better with them once they were older. He went round to the foster home where they spent their whole childhood a few times to try to see them, but thankfully for them he was never allowed access. I heard he even made a pass at their foster mother. I suspect she might have had a bit of a soft spot for him because virtually everyone did when he decided to turn on the charm. He was good at convincing people that his children were the most important things in his life; that he was a dutiful dad who had been wronged by a bad woman and a heartless state.

Although Terry and I didn't get to speak to Chris and Glen again until we were all adults, we did see them a few times just after we were all split up when they were brought to visit the people who lived next door to us. I suppose their foster parents must have been friends of our neighbours. Our front doors were inches away from one another, only divided by a tiny fence, and we could see them coming and going, but we were still ordered by social services not to speak to them. I remember peering out the window, seeing how cute they looked in the nice new clothes their foster mother had bought for them, and just feeling sad. After a while someone must have realized how cruel they were being to all of us by allowing these visits because they suddenly stopped. I didn't see Chris and Glen again after that until I was twenty years old.

Chapter Five

just the three of us

Dad did little more towards looking after Terry and me when he had sole charge of us than he had when Mum was there. We had to feed ourselves most of the time. I would make jam sandwiches if there was any bread in the house, or we'd dig up some spuds from the back garden and make chips. I suppose I'd seen Mum doing these things and I was a fast learner but it's scary to think I was heating a chip pan at such a young age. Dad kept chickens in the back garden, about twenty of them, and they provided us with eggs but they were always escaping and causing problems with the neighbours. I hated those birds, especially the cockerel and the aggressive way it would fly at me, flapping and squawking when I was sent out to collect the eggs. Dad always said his dream was to have a smallholding out in the country where he could be completely self-sufficient but he never did anything about getting one. He never actually did anything about improving any of our lives, just taking refuge from it all in the pubs, hoping to win enough money on the horses to make all his problems go away.

If he hardly ever bothered to feed us, he didn't give a second thought to clothing us; in fact he expected me to help him rather than the other way round. From the moment Mum left I was the one washing and ironing his shirts every day. I'd learnt how to do it by watching Nanny when we visited her bungalow. I had to become good at it because if I made the slightest crease in the wrong place he would give me a slap and shout at me for being stupid, like some eighteenth-century plantation owner overseeing his slaves. But at the same time he would boast to his friends about how wonderful his little girl was, doing all these things for her old man, as if it was evidence of how much I loved him. In a way it was. I felt proud when he talked about me to other people like that but confused that the things he said to my face were completely the opposite. I never knew where I really stood with him, which was one of the ways he kept control in all his relationships and friendships.

Terry and I didn't have any opportunity to wash our own clothes and Dad wasn't worried about how dirty or smelly they became, but he did take an uncomfortable amount of interest in our bath times. He always boasted about how at ease he was with nudity around the house and quite often he would make us have baths with him. The bathroom was off the kitchen, a tiny room containing a sink and a bath that had been crammed in under the slope of the staircase. He'd get in the bath first and then he would call us in when he'd had time for a bit of a soak. Once Terry had washed and got out Dad would tell me to stay and he would sit up on the end with his legs open, ordering me to turn round and look at his naked body while he played with himself.

'I don't want to,' I would protest, staring hard at the taps at the other end, knowing something was wrong with what he was doing but not sure what it was. 'Can't I get out now?' But he would make me stay there until he'd had enough and was ready to get out.

I had long blonde hair, which he was fanatical about, always insistent that I shouldn't have it cut. Every week or two he would wash it for me in the bath and would always rinse it in freezing cold water, laughing as I gasped at the shock of the cold but becoming furious if I cried or made a fuss of any sort. He was like a sadistic little schoolboy sometimes. He had all sorts of mad theories about my hair, like deciding to rinse it in vinegar to give it a shine, and when it came to brushing the knots out he would turn what should have been a pleasant experience for both of us into the most horrifically painful ordeal possible, laughing gleefully all the way through it as I squeaked and squirmed under his brutal tugging.

He had a cruel, warped sense of humour, like a little boy with his practical jokes. When Mum was still with us, he used to pee in the vinegar bottle and watch joyfully as she sprinkled it on her chips. He often used milk bottles to relieve himself in when he was upstairs and couldn't be bothered to come down to the toilet. He would shout for Terry or me to go up and fetch them from him and empty them. If he didn't have a milk bottle handy he would just open the bedroom window and piss through that. He didn't believe any of the rules of normal decent behaviour applied to him; he believed he could do whatever he wanted whenever he wanted.

Dad also seemed to get pleasure from inflicting any sort of pain on people weaker than himself. Sometimes Terry and I would be sitting with him watching television or playing a game quite peacefully and he would suddenly jump up and give one of us a Chinese burn, twisting our little arms as if he was wringing out a wet towel. If we cried out in surprise or pain he would start laughing or would shout at us to 'shut up!' like it was some sort of initiation ceremony designed to toughen us up and we had to be brave.

The unsettling thing was that we could never predict how he would react to anything; sometimes he supported us to an almost lunatic level. He loved his football and one year when Norwich City were in the FA Cup Final, he settled himself down in front of the telly to watch his home team, sending us out into the street to play. Terry got involved in some sort of an argument with another kid and came back indoors crying. Dad was annoyed at having his viewing disturbed but instead of giving Terry a hard time for being a pathetic crybaby, as he normally would have done, he stormed outside to deal with the problem himself. The other lad's dad then also got involved and the two fathers ended up fighting so viciously the police had to be called to separate them. Dad was arrested and taken to the police station. He was angrier about missing the game than anything else. For years afterwards he would tell this story to anyone who would listen, using it as proof of how much he loved his children and how he would always stick up for them when they needed it. But he was unpredictable and Terry and I knew that he could just as easily have laid into him for being a wimp that day and sent him back out into the street to sort it out for himself.

If Terry and I ever started fighting with each other, as we did sometimes like any normal siblings, Dad would urge us to punch properly and not just pull hair or scratch. I remember one time I made Terry's lip bleed with a punch and I felt terrible about it but Dad praised me and wouldn't let Terry hit me back.

I knew never to disobey Dad or to put up an argument about anything. I might ask him to let me off doing something, but if he said no that was the end of it. The moment I heard his voice start to get angry I would always stop pleading because I would know it was hopeless and that if I kept going I was bound to end up being beaten.

Despite being meticulous about his own appearance, Dad didn't care what we went out looking like. We could stink to high heaven and be clad in rags for all he cared. Once a week we would take our dirty washing up to his mother's house, and she would do it all for us so we could pick it back up the following week. One set of clothes always had to last us the whole week, even our socks and underwear. We would take it back and forth between the houses in black bin liners. Terry and I would have to carry the sacks while Dad strode ahead as if he was nothing to do with us. We would try desperately to keep up and if I cried from the pain in my legs he would laugh at how weak I was or become angry with me for complaining. Even Nanny used to tick him off for the state my socks got into, telling him to buy me more clothes so they didn't get so dirty, but he took no notice. No matter how bad they got she always managed to get them clean somehow. My most vivid memory of her is standing at the kitchen sink surrounded by piles of wet washing, scrubbing away like a demon.

It must have been obvious to everyone who saw us or smelled us that we were in a desperate state, and one day the headmistress of the school we were attending decided things had gone far enough and wrote to Dad saying that he needed to 'clean Maria up'. Dad still couldn't read or write so he made me read the letter out loud to him. The idea that anyone else had the right to tell him what to do with his children was impossible for him to grasp. He was absolutely furious that anyone would dare to interfere with the way he ran his family. He might be willing to take that sort of criticism from his own mother, particularly as he needed her to do the washing, but he certainly wasn't going to accept it from someone outside the family setting themselves up as an authority figure.

'You write down what I tell you,' he fumed before starting to dictate a letter to me, which was full of four letter words and graphic insults. At one stage he sent me over the road to ask a neighbour how to spell the word 'whore'. Although I didn't know exactly what it meant, I somehow knew that this wasn't a good thing to be calling my headmistress. I'd heard him use the word often enough when screaming abuse at women or venting his anger at our absent mother, so I knew it was rude.

The neighbour obviously thought it didn't sound right that a child of my age should be asking him such a thing either and came back over with me. Maybe he thought I was trying to wind him up and wanted to check that Dad really had sent me.

'Why does Maria want to know how to spell a word like that?' he asked.

When Dad told him what he was doing the man tried to dissuade him but it didn't work and the next day I had to take the letter in, complete with every expletive copied out in my best neat handwriting. I was mortified because I knew that it wasn't right. I'd always quite liked the headmistress and didn't want to antagonize her, but I was more frightened of angering Dad by not doing as I was told than I was of any teacher.

The letter was delivered and I suppose it was read but nothing further was ever said to me on the matter from either end, and Dad made no more effort to clean me up for school. I guess the headmistress decided that it wasn't a battle worth fighting and Dad put it down as yet another of his famous victories over petty bureaucracy and nosey parkers.

Social services used to give Dad an allowance to take us out and buy clothes but he would just spend it all on drink. When the authorities realized what he was up to they tried giving him vouchers instead but he worked out he could sell them to his friends down the pub for cash. He always had a dozen different schemes going to ensure he had a constant supply of spending money for the pub. Sometimes he put so much effort into trying to get something for nothing that it would have been easier to just have gone out and earned the money he needed, but that wasn't the point for him. The point was to win the game, to get something over on the rest of the world, to show that he was cleverer than everyone else, particularly the people who tried to tell him what to do.

Although he didn't care about Terry and me wearing the same clothes every day he would be very strict about the oddest things, like not chewing bubblegum or not swearing, and he insisted on us polishing our shoes each night. At that time everyone else at school was wearing plimsolls, partly because they were comfortable and partly because it had become a bit of a fashion statement. We used to beg him to let us do the same but he always insisted we wore some proper leather shoes that had been given to us by a kind neighbour. Because we desperately wanted to be like everyone else Terry and I would put our plimsolls in our bags and once we were round the corner from the house we would hurriedly change into them. He must have suspected something was going on because one day he decided to follow us. He caught us red handed and dragged us back home, furious that we were trying to 'get the better of him'. I can't remember what my punishment was, but he forced Terry to wear a great big brightly coloured orange and yellow patterned tie to school. He looked ridiculous and he was crying and sobbing and begging Dad not to make him do it because all the other boys would take the piss, but Dad made him wear it for days on end. Terry was far too scared of what his next punishment might be to be willing to risk disobeying Dad and taking the tie off as soon as he got round the corner. These sorts of intimidations were Dad's way of keeping control of every little aspect of our lives. He loved to humiliate other people in order to demonstrate his own superiority and power over them.

My eyesight as a child was terrible and I went for years without being able to see the blackboard in class properly but not wanting to say anything for fear of drawing attention to myself. Eventually the school picked up on the problem and advised Dad to take me to an optician. He refused to do anything about it, saying I was just pretending not to be able to see in order to get attention. In a way I wasn't too bothered by his reaction because National Health glasses for children were not exactly fashionable in those days and it would have been one more thing making me different to everyone else. I was already a target for some bullies at school and I didn't want to give them yet another reason to pick on me. Eventually one of the children's homes I went into got me glasses while Dad was away on one of his stints in prison and my school-work immediately improved, although my self-esteem sunk a few notches further down the scale.

Although I loved Dad, I realized very early on that our family life wasn't normal because I had occasionally managed to glimpse into other people's lives and knew they were all nicer than ours: there was that nice family the Watsons who fostered us once and then a couple called Ivan Bunn and his wife Ann, who lived a couple of doors up the road from us. They had two daughters called Frances and Denise and a little boy called Stephen, with whom I was very friendly. There was a piano in their house that they let me have a play on whenever Dad let me go round there, which wasn't that often. Although he didn't mind us playing out in the street if it got us out from under his feet, he was always nervous about us becoming too involved with other families. Maybe he was worried we would say too much about what went on behind our closed doors, or that we would realize that life with him wasn't normal. Probably he just didn't like the idea of losing any control over us, of allowing any other adult to have an input into our upbringing or to influence our thinking.

The Bunns must have known that things were tough for us because when I was seven or eight they even invited me on holiday with them to Hemsby, on the Norfolk coast, one summer. I don't know how they got Dad to agree but I was glad they did because it was one of the happiest times of my young life. Ann bought me some pink cotton pyjamas with stripes on the bottom and polka dots on the top and I thought they were the prettiest, softest things I had ever seen. I got sunburnt playing outside during the day and she gently rubbed calamine lotion onto my skin in the evening to try to cool me down and prevent me from peeling. At that moment I felt so cared for and so normal, although all through the holiday I still felt like the odd one out in the group, like an observer merely there to see how a normal family worked. I believed that I didn't deserve to be loved and cherished like the Bunn children were, although I wasn't sure why not. I believed that everything horrible in my life was my own fault; that I was a bad person and didn't deserve any better. I knew that was right because Dad was continually screaming it at me, although I didn't know why or what I should do to become a better, more lovable person.

Many years later, when I was in my thirties, I bumped into Ann when she came into the B & Q store where I was working and we chatted about that holiday all those years ago.

'I've never forgotten that time,' I told her.

'I've got some photographs at home somewhere, and some of you playing in our garden too,' she said. 'I'll pop them in to you if you'd like to see them.'

I was so pleased I could have kissed her, but at the same time I felt a stab of pain to think that this woman, who was really no more than a neighbour, had thought it was worth keeping some photographs of me when my own family had never cared enough to do that. It had always hurt me that no one valued me enough to take any pictures of me and the fact that Ann Bunn had some made me realize all the more how little my own parents had cared for me. When she brought them in a few days later it was like looking at a stranger. I'd had no idea what I looked like when I was small. I was surprised to see that

I was really quite cute, not fat, ugly and unlovable as Dad was always telling me I was.

There were always plenty of new opportunities coming along for Dad to mock and humiliate me. I loved music lessons at school and I enrolled to learn to play the violin. You had to be on a waiting list to be allowed your own instrument and it was a great privilege when you were eventually given one to learn with. When it was finally my turn to be allowed a violin and I was told that I could take it home for a week or two to practise I was thrilled. I felt so proud as I stood in the front room and started playing a few notes for Dad. I was eager for praise and encouragement but instead he just laughed and belittled me.

'You're pathetic,' he sneered. 'You'll never be able to master that.'

And then he grew angry at the noise I was making.

'Don't ever bring that bloody thing home again!'

He never wanted me to do anything that would be outside his control, outside the little world where he was the undisputed king. I desperately wanted to go to Sunday school like my best friend at the time, because it would have been a chance to get out of the house and because I knew the children who attended used to be given milk and biscuits and would come back home with pictures they had painted, but Dad wasn't going to allow that. He was the same about me joining the Brownies or the Guides or doing anything else that other little girls did. It was as if he thought that as a family we were too different and special to behave like everyone else, reinforcing in me the idea that I would never be able to fit in or be as good as everyone else.

There was a lovely church called St Catherine's a few streets from where we lived, which was used by our school for their Christmas and Easter festivities. When I was eight they asked me if I would like to be an angel in the school nativity play and I was over the moon but as usual Dad forbade me from taking part. He didn't give any reason – he didn't feel he had to – and I was left with the feeling that such things were too good for someone like me. Each time I asked to be allowed to do something he would tell me that I wouldn't be capable of it, that I would make a fool of myself, and I believed him. I believed I was useless and didn't deserve to have any of the things other children had or do any of the things they did.

I used to have a recurring nightmare during the years we lived with Dad. I would feel like I was caught in the centre of a spiral of colourful circles. As the spiral gathered speed I would feel trapped, falling faster and deeper into nothingness, certain that if I didn't get out I was going to die. I would try to scream for help but no sounds would come out of my mouth and I would wake up feeling dizzy and nauseous. The nightmares went on for many years, both waking and sleeping.

Chapter Six

upsetting nanny

One winter morning when I was about eight, Dad, Terry and I were relaxing indoors watching television and eating chips. It was snowy outside but the sun was streaming in through the windows and the doors of the coal-burning stove were standing open, making the room feel warm and cosy in the light of the flames. At moments like that I loved our family life, just the three of us together and safe from the outside world in our own home. Eager to maintain the peaceful mood and keep Dad happy I stood up to clear away our plates after eating, thinking I was being a good girl, when something caught my attention on the television. As I watched the screen my concentration slipped for a second, my hand tilted without me noticing and some grease slid off the plate onto the carpet. Dad saw it first and bellowed at me, startling me so much I froze on the spot and the grease continued to flow, making him even angrier, as if I was deliberately disobeying him.

The tranquil mood of a few seconds earlier vanished forever as he leapt from his chair and came at me in a fury, throwing me round the room like a rag doll, sending the plates smashing in all directions, making the mess a hundred times worse. I was terrified as I hurtled through the air that my head would shatter against the walls as easily as the plates.

As his rage became more controlled he snatched up his stick and gave me ten whacks on my bare backside, and still his anger didn't abate. Pushing me aside he stormed upstairs, stripping the blankets off all our beds and scooping up towels wherever they lay. I stood trembling, no idea what was going to happen next but sure I wouldn't like it. He found everything he possibly could that needed washing, forcing it all into two large black bin bags until they bulged at their fragile seams.

'Right,' he shouted when he'd finished, throwing them down at my feet. 'Walk up to Nanny's with that lot.'

I knew exactly how hard it was to carry a single bin liner full of washing that far, I had done it a hundred times over the years, but never two at the same time and never with this much stuffed into them. I knew it was at least a three- or four-mile walk and I could hardly lift the bags they were so heavy. Panic-stricken and unable to stop myself, I burst into tears. I knew from long experience that when he got this angry there was no point arguing with him or pleading, that it would just make him more eager to hit me. I also knew that crying was going to make the situation worse, but I couldn't help it. The logical part of my brain was telling me that I was going to have to do it, so I could choose either to get another beating as well or just get on with it.

He opened the door and pushed me out through it. The cold winter air was a shock after the warmth of the room and I asked if I could get my coat.

'No, you fucking can't,' he roared, 'just get on with it.'

He threw the bags out onto the path and slammed the door behind me. My knees gave way beneath me and I sat down in a crumpled heap, wondering what to do next, knowing that I really only had one option but uncertain if I would be physically strong enough to do it. I was already shaking with cold and sore from the beating. I desperately wanted to go back indoors into the warm, but I knew better than to knock on the door or to beg through the letterbox. There was nothing for it but to accept my punishment and get on with the task he had set me. Pulling myself to my feet I did my best to gather up the huge, slippery sacks and took the first few stumbling steps on my seemingly impossible journey.

It seemed to take forever, the bags getting heavier and more cumbersome with every step. The thin plastic kept splitting wherever I gripped it, making it harder to keep a hold on the escaping laundry and impossible to drag the bags along the ground. I prayed someone in a passing car would see me struggling and offer me a lift, but no one stopped. To distract myself from the pain I devised a game, scoring the houses I passed for their tidiness. Then I set myself little goals to reach between each rest, breaking the journey down into manageable stages. As I passed other people's windows I seemed to see nothing but happy smiling faces and I longed to be inside in the warm with them, to be part of a normal family where everyone was nice to one another. I knew I didn't deserve to be that happy because Dad was always telling me so, shouting at me about how bad I was and how it was all my fault Mum had gone away, but that didn't stop me from fantasizing about it.

When I finally fell in through Nanny's front door she was obviously shocked by the state of me and by the flimsy clothes I'd been sent out in. When I told her what had happened, expecting her to be cross with me for spilling the grease on the floor too, she was remarkably sympathetic. Normally I would have expected her to give me a telling off as well, maybe even an extra clip round the ear for good measure. Having someone be kind to me opened the floodgates and I couldn't stop crying. Although she still didn't cuddle me, because she never could bring herself to do that, she did at least sit me down and make me a hot drink, assuring me everything would be all right, and that she would sort Dad out. She rang him in front of me and gave him a good telling off for what he had made me do. It felt so nice to have someone actually speaking up for me, although as I listened I wished she would stop before she made him even angrier with me. I knew I was going to have to go back soon and I didn't want him to be waiting at the door with the stick again. My backside was still stinging from the previous thrashing.

I had such a lovely afternoon with Nanny I didn't want to go home, but she assured me Dad wouldn't hit me any more, and even gave me some money so I could take the bus back. I left her bungalow weighed down with two carrier bags full of groceries and another bin liner full of clean laundry from the previous week. I was pretty sure Dad would be pleased with the free food and that going through the bags would calm him down a bit and maybe even make him forget how angry he was with me. I started to feel a little better as I sat on the bus, although still apprehensive about what I might have to face when I walked in through the front door.

It had been an exhausting day and I must have closed my eyes for a second in the warmth of the bus and drifted off. When I opened them I realized I'd missed my stop and immediately panicked. I didn't want to have to walk miles back with all Nanny's bags when every muscle in my body was still aching from the first trip. I hauled myself out of my seat and lurched down the moving bus to the platform at the back, waiting for an opportunity to get off. When the driver slowed down at some traffic lights I took a chance and jumped. As I stumbled onto the cold pavement, landing in a heap, one of Nanny's carrier bags split open. I stared in dismay at a bag of sugar that had exploded across the pavement, mingling with the snow and slush. I felt physically sick at the sight of what I had done. How was I going to tell Dad that I had made yet another clumsy mistake? He would be utterly furious that I had wasted a whole bag of free sugar.

I sat on the ground for what seemed like ages, wondering what to do, just wanting the pavement to open up and swallow me. I even considered turning round and running away, leaving all the bags where they had fallen rather than facing his wrath yet again; but I couldn't think of anywhere to run to. I could hardly go back to Nanny's now that I had spilled her sugar and I didn't have any money left for another bus anyway. There was no option but to go into the house and face the music.

As I packed everything back into the bags I thought maybe I would be able to get away with it since Dad had no idea what had been in them when Nanny first sent me off. I decided to just pretend nothing had happened and hope for the best.

The moment I came through the door Dad told me he'd been on the phone to Nanny, asking when I would be home. She'd told him she was sending groceries and he'd asked exactly what she was sending. My heart sank as he told me this while he unpacked the bag greedily, praying that he wouldn't miss the sugar.

'Where's the sugar?' he demanded.

Panic overwhelmed me and I lied before I could stop myself. 'Nanny didn't give us any sugar.'

'She told me she did.'

Dad was determined to get to the bottom of the mystery. He did not intend to be cheated out of a free bag of sugar. I desperately wanted to take back my lie and tell him the truth but I'd left it too late and become trapped by my own panicked words. I'd made things even worse for myself because now if I was found out I would be in trouble both for spilling the sugar and for lying. It would have been so much better to have owned up from the beginning and taken my punishment – after all I deserved it, didn't I?

If I kept quiet, I reasoned, maybe he would get bored with the whole argument and forget about it. But he didn't. He was short of one bag of sugar and he intended to find out what had happened to it. Was it his daughter trying to pull the wool over his eyes or his mother? He rang Nanny back and they were arguing about whether or not she had put sugar in the bag. She was insisting she put it in while he was insisting she hadn't and was calling her a liar. I felt terrible, the pressure was building inside my head until I couldn't bear it any longer and I blurted out the truth.

'I had an accident! I fell over and the sugar broke.'

I immediately felt a weight lifting off my conscience. I knew I would be punished, and I was terrified of what form that punishment might be going to take, but at least I had told the truth. To my surprise he didn't go quite as mad as I had expected him to. He almost seemed to be pleased to discover the truth. My breathing began to come a little more easily. I had learned a valuable lesson, I told myself, and I now knew that if I lied I would inevitably be found out. But in learning the lesson I had earned myself the title of 'liar'. As well as giving my father the evidence he needed when he wanted to prove to me that I was a bad girl and that no one other than him would ever love me, I had also alienated Nanny after we had spent such a nice time together and she had been so kind to me. With that one lie I had given both her and my father a weapon they could use against me for years. I had proved how unworthy of their love I was.

As a child, I had always got the sense that Nanny didn't like me, because she was always giving me clips on the ear and telling me off. I think maybe I annoyed her when I was little, always looking for approval, and she certainly didn't take any lip from me. That's why it was a surprise when she was kind that day when Dad sent me up there with the laundry. I suppose she could see that he had overstepped the mark, sending a young girl out in the snow with scarcely any clothes on. It could have been a chance to make her change her mind about me and instead I had blown it all by telling that stupid lie.

Even though I had let myself down in her eyes, I was still included with the family when we went up to her house for lunch on Sundays. I liked going because her meals were always great, with puddings and everything, and Terry and I would stuff ourselves as much as possible. I used to watch everything Nanny did, trying to learn so I could look after Dad at home in the same way. She made the best cheese on toast in the world, standing a loaf of bread cut side up on the table, putting the cheese on first and then cutting a perfect slice horizontally. It meant the bread didn't fall apart and seemed incredibly clever to me. Little things like that sometimes stick in the memories of children more firmly than the big things.

I had four cousins on Dad's side and Nanny often used to look after them during the week while their parents were at work, but she never offered to look after us even though we obviously needed her help. Maybe Dad didn't want her to, but I suspect it's more likely she never offered. Why would she allow Chris and Glen to stay in care rather than have them with her? Why couldn't she see that Dad wasn't looking after us properly and do something about it? The questions went round and round in my head but there was no one I could turn to for any answers, especially not her, so I just stored all the hurt up inside.

I think some of Dad's family did try to help us out in the beginning. Dad's sister Jill, who would sometimes be at Nanny's at the weekends, bought us Christmas presents one year, knowing Dad wouldn't get round to it. I remember she gave me a little plastic cash register that I loved playing shops with, and Terry got a set of plastic cowboy and Indian figures. Jill's husband, who had his own decorating business, used to offer to give Dad a job, but Dad never bothered to take him up on the offer so eventually they both seemed to give up on us totally. I think that's what happened with all our relatives; our problems were so huge that they couldn't see a solution and they just kind of gave up on us.

My cousins were always quite kind to me but I was too shy to know how to respond to their attempts to include me in their games. We would play together in the empty house next door to Nanny's but it was awkward for me. They had such posh accents I never felt good enough and I always felt different to them all.

Nanny might have been keen for Dad to marry Mum at the beginning, but once Mum had gone Nanny did nothing but slag her off for being a terrible mother and for dumping her four children. She never got over the shame of having one of her grandchildren found eating the contents of his nappy, which wasn't surprising.

However much I disliked hearing her being horrible about my mum, I couldn't really argue since I agreed with most of what she said. I was furious with her for leaving us as well. But it still wasn't nice for Terry and me to have to listen to the constant harangue.

None of us had heard a single word from Mum since she'd gone, not a birthday card or a Christmas card or anything, so we didn't need our Nan to be continually reminding us how hurt we felt and how badly we had been let down. She didn't blame Dad for any of it, although it was mainly due to him that Christian and Glen were locked in their bedroom and ignored, sometimes for days on end, and it was him who had forced Mum out onto the streets and made her life so unbearable she felt she had no choice but to leave. Dad was never in the wrong for anything as far as Nanny was concerned. Whatever he did that she disapproved of, like drinking too much or not working, she put down to the fact that his cruel wife had deserted him and broken his heart. She'd tell him off herself sometimes, but she wouldn't hear anyone else criticizing him without sticking up for him.

I sometimes wonder if she was also jealous of my close relationship with her beloved son. Could that explain why she seemed to take against me from an early age? Whatever the reason, she never missed a chance to give me a slap in passing. It wasn't systematic beatings like

Dad handed out, but however hard Dad hit me I always knew he loved me, because he told me so and because he was still there for me. Nanny would never have told me that she loved me and I was completely convinced she didn't. Sometimes she was just behaving like a lot of women of that generation did when it came to disciplining children. I used to bite my nails, for instance, and whenever she caught me she would give me a whack round the back of the head. If it had always been for specific things like that I might have understood it, even if I didn't like it, but wherever I was in the bungalow I always seemed to be in her way, particularly in her tiny kitchen, and would always get a slap for it. I didn't question it at the time because I thought she must be right, that I must deserve every slap she gave me. I was very shy and convinced that I was in everyone's way anyway. I knew I couldn't be any good otherwise why would my mother have left me and why would my dad have to beat me so often?

Now, as an adult, I think that maybe part of the reason why Nanny hated me was because I reminded her of Mum, the woman who had reputedly ruined her son's life. In the end I fulfilled all her worst thoughts and feelings about me by betraying my father as completely as Mum had done – at least that would be how Nanny came to see it.

Chapter Seven

dad's broken heart

Dad never truly recovered from the shock of Mum walking out on him. Partly that may have been because he had lost his main source of income, but there is no doubt he also believed he had lost the love of his life and would never be able to replace her. Every night he would go out drinking to drown his sorrows – although he probably would have done the drinking anyway because he was already doing it before Mum left; his broken heart merely gave him another excuse.

He never thought to hire babysitters when he was out, so if he didn't take us with him Terry and I would sit waiting for him to come home at night. Even if we grew tired and decided to go up to bed we wouldn't be able to sleep, worrying that Dad might have been involved in an accident or a fight, or was so drunk he couldn't find his way back to us. I felt responsible for him. We knew that if something happened to Dad we would be orphans with no family left to look after us since none of our other relatives were showing much interest. We wished he would take better care of himself as well as of us, so we could feel safer.

When we did eventually hear him falling in through the front door after closing time we would hurry back downstairs to greet him because we knew he liked that. If we had by any chance fallen asleep he would stumble upstairs to wake us so that he could weep to us uncontrollably about his lost love, falling on his knees, sobbing to the gods. He always needed to have an audience for the drama of his grief.

'Jane, Jane,' he would wail, 'please, please come back.' He would go on like that for hours some nights and there was nothing either of us could do or say that would offer him any relief from his misery.

If we tried to sneak away back to bed during one of these performances he would go mad at us, determined that we should witness his torment in full and appreciate what a wicked selfish bitch our mother was. It was confusing: I hated her for what she had done to all of us, but I still wanted her to come back for his sake, and for Terry's. I kept thinking, why doesn't this woman just come back? Not for me because I didn't care, but for him, my poor demented father, as I watched him pleading, begging the gods, banging his head on the floor, beside himself with grief. As I watched him punching the air and crying I would hate her even more but at the same time I remember wishing he would shut up about it and get on with his life with us.

He was the same wherever he went. Down the pub they all thought he was amazing for soldiering on alone after Mum had deserted him and the social services had taken away half his children. He spent hours telling anyone who would listen all about his woes. He would tell them of his struggle to get us out of care and regale them with the story of how he had beaten up the social worker who refused to let him see his children. He used to play the same record on the jukebox, that one by Charlie Rich, 'Hey, did you happen to see the most beautiful girl in the world, and if you did, was she crying?' It was all about how a man had let the love of his life go and now realized his mistake, but too late to do anything about it. The lyrics fitted the picture that he held in his head of what had happened and he played the same track over and over again, standing by the jukebox, tears streaming down his face, singing along like his heart was breaking all over again. I learned to hate the sound of that record. Just hearing the first few chords striking up would make my heart sink. Why did he always have to think about her? Why was he always pining for her, when he had me and I was willing to do anything to make him happy?

When we were all at home together during the day Dad had a little routine going. To help him elicit sympathy from everyone in the pub he liked to take one of us with him wherever he went, like a little trophy to show what a good father he was, part of his act like Pussy the corgi. Usually it was me who went because Terry wasn't quite as co-operative and for some reason he was more willing to let Terry off these duties than me. His money always arrived on the same days. He would be paid his income support for keeping us on a Monday and on a Tuesday he would get his child benefit payment. The Post Office, where the money came from, didn't open till nine o'clock in the mornings and he couldn't bring himself to queue like everyone else, so I would have to go to do his queu- ing for him, which meant that on those days I was too late for registration at school so I could then spend the rest of the day with him, or at least I could spend it sitting out- side whichever pub he had decided to take his money to, waiting for him to come out.

Sometimes I'd be there for hours on end. The pubs had embossed windows that you couldn't see through but whenever anyone went in or came out through the doors, I'd peer in trying to get a glimpse inside to look for Dad and check what he was doing.

Dad's friends kept telling Terry and me how wonderful our dad was and how grateful we should be to have such a great father and that we should make sure we behaved for him and didn't make his life any more difficult than it was. I was sick of hearing it all, especially as I always felt guilty for being the bad, inferior person that Dad was constantly telling me I was. I remember two old ladies coming out of the pub one time after listening to Dad's sob story, both of them in tears and bearing gifts of crisps and Coke, telling me what a wicked woman our mother was.

'You be a good girl for your poor daddy,' they said as they handed over their gifts.

At moments like that I felt that my dad really was a hero for all he was doing for us, and Mum really was the villain of our story. Poor Dad. He needed to drink to dim the pain of his broken heart.

When he couldn't bear to have Mum's clothes and wigs in the house for a moment longer he built a bonfire out the back and burned the lot, like a mock funeral pyre. He used to have some photos of her as well, which he kept on the top shelf of the pantry, but they disappeared too, went missing one time when he was in prison and the council repossessed the house, forcing us to move. But it didn't matter what happened to the physical reminders of her; he was never going to forget her, or let anyone else forget that the love of his life had walked out on him.

There was one publican who used to feel sorry for me and ask if I would like to go up and sit in his living quarters above the pub rather than always waiting out in the cold. Sometimes Dad would agree but mostly he would say no. 'She'll be all right outside,' he'd say dismissively, not wanting to be beholden to anyone.

It was confusing. If he was as wonderful a father as everyone told us, how come there was never any food in the house? How come he never went shopping for us? How come he never went to work to support us all? How come he didn't make our bedrooms habitable or buy us birthday cards or cuddle us when we cried? How come he beat us so often when we hadn't done anything really bad? It's only looking back that I question all this, though. At the time I never thought it was unusual that he spent all his money in the pub and behaved the way he did; that's just the way things were, it's what I was used to.

Dad hated the idea of buying anything in the normal way from the shops. He would never have belittled himself to walk around a supermarket with a basket and buy things over the counter like everyone else; he would rather we just went without. There was never any breakfast in the house when Terry and I got up. Some mornings on the way to school I would strip the leaves off bushes and pull up stalks of grass just to give myself something to chew on to stave off the pangs of hunger. Some of these things used to taste surprisingly nice and juicy but they never did much for the hunger pains. After school Terry and I used to wait outside the chippy at the bottom of our road, tortured by the delicious smells of frying and going in every so often to ask for 'the crispies', which were the scrapings from the frying vats.

We were always moaning at Dad for not going shopping so one day, after he'd had a win on the horses, he gave us five pounds each to shop with. 'That means you can't eat any of my potatoes or eggs,' he warned. 'I'm not feeding you for a week, you can sort yourselves out if you're so bloody clever.'

Terry and I thought this was wonderful and headed straight down to the shop to buy ourselves a big box of cereal and milk and sugar, bread and jam and butter, all the things that were never usually in the house. Within a few days we had to go to him and admit that we'd messed up. We'd spent all the money and eaten everything we'd bought. He wasn't angry because he liked being proved right. Our failure had demonstrated that we couldn't manage without him and gave him another opportunity to mock our feeble efforts at being independent.

Because there was never a meal ready for us when we got home in the evenings, whenever Terry and I managed to go to school we would make sure we ate everything on offer for lunch, always going up for second helpings. Every so often, however, that would backfire on us and we would get home to find Dad had decided to come off the drink and had suddenly transformed into the perfect father. Where usually Terry and I did all the housework, we would come through the door and find him on his hands and knees scrubbing the house from top to bottom, or stripping wallpaper or painting something while cooking an enormous meal for us at the same time, usually a sausage and potato casserole, or sausage, mash and peas. I would be so proud of him when that happened and would tell all my friends at school the next day that my dad had given up drinking and loved me just as much as their dads loved them.

Because we never had any warning of when these mood changes would happen, however, we were often stuffed full with school lunch and unable to do justice to the food he was proudly laying out in front of us, which would lead to another explosion of temper. He would rant on about how ungrateful we were and how he slaved for us. Under his watchful eyes I would force myself to keep eating, pushing in mouthful after mouthful, even though each one was making me feel sick, just to avoid making him angry or hurting his feelings. Sometimes these 'perfect father' phases lasted a few days and Terry and I would decide to skip school lunches to ensure we still had our appetites by the time we got home, but the first day that would happen we would get in to find he was back down the pub. We would be starving, the cupboard would be bare once more and we would know there was going to be nothing until school lunch the following day.

Other days when we came home from school we would still find no food in the kitchen but the house would be full of his hangers-on, people he had brought home from the pub with him. They were nearly always alcoholics or prostitutes and they were often taking refuge in our house because they were in some sort of trouble and needed a place to go. Dad would never turn anyone in need away; he was always the first one to invite someone in and offer them a couch to sleep on if they came to him with any sort of sob story. He liked people to be dependent on him and grateful to him for being such a great guy, although he would turn on them in a second if he thought they were starting to take liberties or were taking him for granted.

I remember a couple of Christmases when for some strange reason he decided to make an enormous effort for us. To start with he would buy a box of After Eights because they were 'your mum's favourites'. I hated the bloody things, partly because I knew it would mean he would get all emotional and upset as he ate them and we would have to listen to him reminiscing about her again and moaning on about his broken heart. He never stopped talking about her for long and any woman he went out with always knew that she came second to 'his Jane'.

'She's all right,' he'd say about any girlfriend who was on the scene, 'but no one will ever measure up to my Jane.'

He made sure we had enough food for a proper Christmas lunch for the three of us by spending days beforehand plucking turkeys in the kitchen and in the bathroom for a mate of his, thus earning some extra money to buy the food we needed. His fingers would be bleeding from the work and every time that happened I would be convinced he had changed. At moments like that it would be hard to be angry with him for the way he behaved on the other three hundred and sixty days of the year. If he had decided to change the way he behaved at any stage we would have forgiven him for whatever might have happened before, putting it down to the effect of Mum leaving. But if anything his behaviour grew worse over the years, not better, and the little respites became fewer and further between.

When the pubs closed at two thirty in the afternoon, Dad would make his way to the bookies, scooping me up from wherever I had been waiting outside. I would trot obediently in his wake like a nervous puppy desperate for approval, desperate not to be left behind. He wouldn't talk to me much before disappearing into the bookies and I would know that I had to wait outside again, staring into shop windows at nice clothes and toys, or gazing longingly at any food on display, always hungry, always imagining that one day he might come out with enough winnings to decide to buy me something to eat, but knowing deep inside that he would never do that, no matter how much he won. Sometimes, when he did finally emerge, I would try to hold his hand as he strode off.

'Don't be silly,' he would scold, brushing me aside, 'people will think you're my girlfriend.' Holding hands with a child would have made him look soft, I suppose, whereas he thought having me trailing along behind him made him look cool in some way.

How well he did at the bookies would determine what sort of mood he would be in for the rest of the day and we would either be taking a taxi home or he would be walking and I would be running to keep up. I sometimes tried to ask him how much he had won or lost, but he always ignored the questions, as though I didn't exist, as though I wasn't worth talking to.

On the way home we would sometimes walk past a men's public toilet and Dad used to tell me to wait again while he disappeared inside. I could never understand why he took so long in there as I sat on the wall outside watching other men coming and going. Eventually he would come strutting back out and I noticed that he often then had enough money to get us a taxi for the rest of the journey. It was only years later that it occurred to me what might have been going on inside that toilet while I waited. If he thought all women were 'sitting on a gold-mine' and should exploit it, maybe he felt the same about himself.

If he had no money at all but he had decided to make egg and chips for tea he would send me into the little supermarket we passed on the way home to nick some sausages or bacon to go with it. I was terrified of being caught, but I was more terrified of the consequences of disobeying him. He would make Terry do it too, but

Terry wasn't as good at it as I was, more nervous. Maybe the shopkeepers kept a closer eye on him, being a boy and a year older. I used to just shove things under my coat and head for the exit and never seemed to get caught. I was quite proud of my skill and always hoped it would make Dad be nicer to me.

But his moods were largely unpredictable. Sometimes when he got fed up with Terry or me at home he would lock one or other of us in the coal shed, which was just off the kitchen and was rarely full of coal. I think I was about seven the first time it happened, soon after Mum left. Most often he would do it for no apparent reason at all, just because he felt like it. To begin with I would plead with him as he dragged me closer and closer to the door.

'Daddy, please don't, I'll be good, I promise, please don't, Daddy. I love you, Daddy. I'm sorry.'

But he would just laugh at my pleading or simply ignore it. He never relented once he had decided he was going to punish us. He would have seen that as showing weakness, which he would never have been able to do. Once we were inside with the door locked behind us, sitting in the dark and cold on whatever coal was in there, we didn't dare to call out or make any sound at all. It was so black that it didn't make any difference whether you kept your eyes open or shut. I would sit huddled in the corner with my legs drawn up close to my chest and wait, my ears straining for any sound. Were there snakes in there? I wondered. Were there rats or mice that would eat me before anyone came to save me? Hearing noises from the normal world outside the door like a telephone ringing or a door closing or Dad's voice would give me hope, reminding me that I was only in a coal shed and that I would eventually be released.

Sometimes once he had silenced us in the shed Dad would fall asleep in his chair and forget we were even in the house, leaving us alone in the dark for hours at a time. Eventually he would wake up in a drunken stupor, amble to the coal shed door and seem surprised to find us still sitting there. If I had been in the blackness a long time the sudden light would hurt my eyes when it finally arrived.

Neither Terry nor I ever dared to intervene when the other one was being locked up because we knew that we would suffer a worse punishment if we did. It was tempting sometimes to go and unbolt the door when I knew he was locked in the shed and I know he felt the same thing when I was in there, but the beating we'd have got from Dad just wouldn't have been worth it. In every other way, Terry and I stuck together – him and me against the outside world – but we never had the courage to gang together and stand up to Dad.

It was always up to one of us to fetch the coal from the shop because such a menial task would have been beneath Dad's dignity. The merchant wouldn't deliver it to the house because Dad never paid his bills, so he used to send us down the hill to the shop to buy it and we would have to carry it back up on our shoulders.

But these punishments and humiliations would have been bearable if that was all he had done to us. I could have found excuses and forgiven him for all of them if it wasn't for what he started to do to me next.

Chapter Eight

reading to dad

One of the things Dad liked us to do was read the evening paper to him each day when he got back from the pub because he couldn't do it for himself. He'd look at the pictures and ask us what the headlines were saying. If they interested him then he would tell us to read on. I suppose it was quite good practice for us, although some of the words were hard. I remember having trouble getting my head round the way they spelled jail 'gaol'.

Believe it or not, that was how the next level of abuse started, with me reading to my father. He had a collection of pornographic magazines and he would order me upstairs the moment he walked in through the front door, usually when he was fuelled up with drink, but not always. He would get me to sit on the edge of the bed and read explicit stories to him while he lay beside me and masturbated. Not that I realized that was the name for what he was doing; I was only eight or nine years old at the time. I didn't understand what he was doing to himself at all, any more than I understood any of the things that I was having to read out to him – I just knew that none of it felt right and I didn't like it. To begin with I would beg him not to make me do it and I would be unable to stop the tears from flowing, but then he would become angry and shout and I would be terrified of what he might do if I didn't keep reading. There was no reasoning with him when he was in that frame of mind and I knew I had no choice but to obey. It was preferable to taking a beating from the slipper or the stick. I would try not to look at him or what he was doing, although it was impossible to ignore the shaking of the bed beneath us, and I would try not to focus on the pictures in the magazines either, concentrating on the words on the page and trying to block out everything else. I just wanted the whole thing to be over as quickly as possible.

Then he started making me lie down next to him while I read and he would reach across with his spare hand to play around with me inside my knickers, which made me feel uncomfortable and fearful even though it didn't hurt to start with.

After it was all over he would give me a big lecture each time about not telling anyone what we did together. He would tell me about a little girl we knew from down the road whose daddy had gone to prison because she told stories about him.

'If I go to prison you and Terry will be sent to a children's home and everyone will hate you,' he would warn. 'Children's homes are full of perverts who will torture you and rape you. You need to have your daddy here to protect you. You're fat and you're ugly and no one except me is ever going to love you.'

I believed him completely. Even though I hated the things he did I still didn't want him to go back to prison. We were a family and I wanted us to be together. His stories about children's homes were terrifying, even though I had never had that bad a time myself whenever we had been taken into one. I always thought that the next one we went to might be where all the terrible things he described would happen. As the level of his interference with me escalated he kept saying there was no point in telling anyone what was happening between us anyway, because they would never believe me.

'This is our secret,' he'd tell me. 'No one will believe anything you say until you're ten anyway.'

Later, when he was finally called to answer for what he had done to me, he claimed that I had misunderstood what he was doing, that it was just that he had an 'open' attitude to nudity and sex. That was certainly true in that he saw nothing wrong with doing whatever he wanted, but that didn't mean I liked it. No child wants their parents to walk around the house with no clothes on or to pee out the windows or fiddle around inside their knickers.

Once I'd realized there was no point in asking him to stop during these sessions or in attempting to run away, I tried to let him get on with it and concentrate on other things, pretending to myself that it wasn't happening, hoping it would all be over as quickly as possible. I convinced myself that maybe it wasn't so terrible. Then one day, when I was still only about nine, he came in from the pub as usual and asked if I wanted a lollipop.

'Yes please, Daddy,' I replied eagerly.

As he took my hand and marched me upstairs I felt confused. Surely there weren't any lollies up there and I hadn't heard the ice cream van in the street outside. My heart sank as he gave me a magazine and lay down on the bed to masturbate as usual. I guessed the offer of a lolly had been one of his unkind jokes but after a few minutes he asked again.

'Do you want a lollipop then?'

'Yes,' I said, hoping that would mean he had finished relieving himself. 'Where are they?'

'Come here,' he said and as I leaned across he grabbed my head. 'Suck this!'

Before I knew what was happening he had forced himself into my mouth and I felt like I was suffocating. As I instinctively struggled to get away he became angry. Tears were streaming down my face and I was gagging and choking, certain he was going to kill me. I couldn't breathe because his thing was so huge. He kept thrusting it further and further down my throat, pushing harder on the back of my head, impaling me so I couldn't pull away. There was no way I could think of other things while this was going on. There was no escape either physically or mentally from this new torture.

Eventually he let me go and just lay there laughing at me. I felt so stupid for allowing him to trick me with the promise of a lollipop. What had made me think for a single second that he would have given me a treat for no reason? Why did I still hold out the hope that he would want to be kind to me, at least occasionally?

Once I could breathe again I also felt foolish for thinking I was going to die a few minutes before, wondering if perhaps I had been making a fuss about nothing. If Dad thought it was just a joke maybe it wasn't such a big deal after all. I hated him and loved him and felt sorry for him and for myself all at the same time. I always made excuses for him when he drank but I couldn't find any excuses for him doing that to me; it was too disgusting and too frightening.

When he started trying to have penetrative sex with me I was even more terrified and convinced I was going to die. His horrible fat thing was so big I thought it was going to split me in two as he tried to force it in between my legs. I imagined my whole body would tear in half and I would dissolve into nothingness. He was huge, drunk and awful at moments like that. He smelled vile, this great heavy man lying on top of me, trying to jab his way into me, not caring if I screamed and cried from the pain. I was certain something terrible was going to happen to me.

He licked his fingers to wet me down below. 'This'll make it easier,' he said.

'Please, don't!' I pleaded, over and over again.

'Just relax,' he said, taking no notice of my sobbing. 'Stop making such a bloody fuss and it'll be over a lot quicker and it won't hurt so much.'

I'd try to do as he told me because I wanted it over as quickly as possible. I knew there was no point fighting because of the size of him. He was so big and strong and because he was my daddy I believed him when he said I had to do it. I suppose it was like when a parent tells a child they have to take a nasty-tasting medicine the doctor has prescribed, or that they need to roll up their sleeve for a painful injection because in the long run it may save their life. I knew that some things have to be done just because the grown-ups say so. I assumed this must be one of those things because that was what he told me.

I wished he didn't smell so bad though. He would have started the day by showering and shampooing and dousing himself in Brut or Old Spice but by the time he had spent a long day in the pub those smells were drowned out by the stale stink of smoke and alcohol that clung to his skin and his breath and his hair, filling my nostrils and making me feel sick.

Once he'd finished he would always laugh at me. 'See, it wasn't that bad, was it?'

There wouldn't have been any point in telling him just how terrible it had been because either he wouldn't have believed me or he would have been angered by my ingratitude for all he did for me.

After the first time, he said, 'Now you've done it once you can start doing it for money.' His words filled me with dread, even though I didn't quite understand what he meant and even though he didn't actually do anything about it at that stage. If it hurt this much when he did it, surely he couldn't mean to make me do it with other men? I hoped with all my heart that wasn't what he meant.

Once he knew he could get away with penetrating me, he wanted to do it all the time. Sometimes it seemed as though he was deliberately trying to court danger, as if taking the risk of getting caught was part of the thrill for him, showing that he wasn't frightened of anyone, that he was above the law and could do whatever he wanted. There was a scrubby piece of woodland sandwiched between two roads in Norwich and a couple of times he detoured and deliberately took me in there on our way back from the pubs and the betting shops. There were cars roaring past just a few yards either side of us while he was attempting to fuck me, like he was daring the outside world to try to stop him doing whatever he wanted. I couldn't understand why he didn't just wait a few more minutes until we got home, but I would never have found the courage to ask. I was still just running around behind him like a little puppy, eager to please him in any way I could, always hoping not to be hurt too much in the process, terrified of being rejected. I'd given up expecting any affection a long time ago.

Always looking for new ways to make easy money, Dad did up our bedrooms a bit and got a string of lodgers in, moving Terry and me into his room to share a bed with him, a situation that we both hated but dared not complain about. He would make me sleep next to him because he said Terry kicked too much in his sleep. I was always frightened when he was lying next to me, but it was worse if I knew he'd been drinking and would be wanting to feel me up with Terry asleep on the other side of me. It was still disgusting to me even once Dad had fallen asleep and I never got used to the stale smell of alcohol wafting across the pillow into my face as he snored away.

When Mum walked out and he lost her income, money had become really tight. It certainly didn't occur to him to work himself and he had to rely on coming up with new scams the whole time just to survive. When he got awarded custody of Terry and me as a single parent he gloated to anyone who would listen that he would never have to work again because our child benefits would be his meal ticket. It wasn't long before he realized he needed more than our benefit cheques to maintain a drinking habit as generous as his.

As well as paying him rent, some of the lodgers provided him with yet another source of income because their giros would come to the house and he would nick them off the doormat before they saw them. He would then get me to forge their signatures and take the giros up to a post office in another area of the city to get the cash. It only happened a few times before the police came round and took a specimen of Dad's writing to match it up to the signatures. It didn't occur to them to take a sample of my writing. Who would expect a shy little nine-year-old girl to be forging giros?

'You can't get done for this,' Dad would assure me if I got nervous and asked if I would be sent to prison, 'because you're not legally responsible until you're ten years old.'

Most of the lodgers only stayed a few days at a time and often they left because Dad had picked a fight with them. The only ones that I can remember clearly were two young lads, one of whom was really good-looking and sweet. Terry and I were sitting with him one afternoon talking and eating a packet of chocolate biscuits that

Nanny had dropped round the day before, when Dad arrived home. Any sort of biscuits were a bit of a rarity in our house and we certainly never had chocolate ones as a rule so I think Terry and I had assumed they belonged to the lodgers. Dad must have been looking forward to a chocolate biscuit with his tea all the way home and when he saw what was happening he exploded. He took all his anger out on the lodger, beating the guy to a pulp in front of us, splattering the sitting room in his blood as he punched and kicked and threw him around, accusing him of stealing his biscuits. Terry and I tried to explain it was our fault but he wouldn't listen. He got together all the lodger's stuff and hurled it out into the street. Even though I was only little I remember wondering why he would react so violently over a packet of biscuits when all he had to do was buy another one. Looking back now I realize it may have been because he saw I liked the boy and he felt there was a threat to his total control of the home. He wouldn't have wanted Terry and me to have any heroes other than him. I felt so guilty about the punishment that lad suffered, certain as always that it was all my fault.

Another lodger left the front gate open and our dog got lost, so he got a beating too before being thrown out onto the street. It was as though Dad had a problem with having any rival males on his patch, even when they were paying him rent.

It was never possible to predict his reactions to anything. Sometimes he would explode over something that no one else had noticed and at other times we would be shaking in our boots in anticipation of a bad reaction and he would be fine. It all added to our insecurity and increased his power over us, keeping us off balance and nervous all the time. He had a certificate framed on the lounge wall that was something to do with him being a member of the freemasons. It was his pride and joy and when Terry and I smashed the glass one day playing ball indoors we both thought we were going to be dead meat when he got home. There was no way we could do anything to disguise the breakage or mend it so we were quaking with fear by the time he came through the door, both of us apologizing and begging for mercy.

'Don't worry about it,' he grinned as if we were silly to make a fuss about something so trivial. 'We can always get some new glass.'

Working on his favourite principle that we were too young to be arrested, he sent Terry and me out shoplifting for him more and more frequently. It might have started with us being instructed to bring back just a packet of bacon or some other much-needed food, but he soon developed a habit of ordering us to steal bottles of whisky that he could share out with his mates. As he was handing the whisky round at home he would be boasting to them about his clever little shoplifting daughter as though I'd just won a prize. I would burst with pride as he sung my praises and his mates would stare at me in amazement, not realizing that I only did it because he forced me to. If only he could have been as proud of me when I played the violin or did well at school.

I always seemed to get away with nicking the whisky for him. I suppose it never occurred to the shopkeepers that a little girl would do that sort of thing so they didn't bother to watch me too carefully when I went to that area of the shop. To make it even more difficult he was always really particular about the brands he would accept. It had to be Teachers or White Horse. Sometimes he would come out on these raids with us himself, acting like a ring master. There was a bicycle that was always parked in the same place round the back of the supermarket, with a satchel behind the saddle. He would stand beside it and take the bottles from me, sending me straight back in for more, storing them in the satchel until I had brought him three or four, then he would fish them out and we would head home triumphantly. He thought it was brilliant that he had trained me like this, feeling he was outwitting the law. Although I hated having to steal, I was proud to think that I had finally found a way to please him and show him I wasn't completely useless.

One time when he sent Terry and me out to steal whisky on our own we decided we would pinch some sweets instead, since we were hungry as usual, and that was the one time we were caught. I guess shopkeepers watch more carefully when kids are hovering around the sweets counter than around the off licence shelves. Although I was terrified of what was going to happen to us when the police were called, there was a part of me that was relieved because I thought that now we had been caught Dad would realize he shouldn't send us out any more, that it was too risky. When the police took us home and told him what had happened he put on a great act of being the outraged parent, assuring them that he would be giving us both a hiding and would be making sure we never did such a terrible thing again, calling us 'the little sods'. I hated it when he behaved like that, all his bravado gone, just craven and cowardly and lying to save his own skin.

Once the police had gone he was even more furious with us, not because of the dishonesty, obviously, and not because we had got ourselves caught, although he saw that as more evidence of how useless we were, but because we had disobeyed him and gone for the sweets rather than the whisky. He sent us straight back out again to make good our mistake.

'Don't come back until you've each got a bottle for me,' he ordered.

Terry was in floods of tears by then, certain that he just couldn't go back out there after everything we had already been through that day, so I had to do it for both of us. I never minded doing things for Terry because he was always kind to me when he had a chance. We were in this together.

Dad would hide the bottles we brought home under the settee, delighted yet again at the idea of getting something for nothing, bringing them out when his friends arrived so they could spend the nights drinking and playing cards. The fact that they had come free added to the pleasure he took in them. His aversion to paying for anything meant that he didn't even like buying toilet paper, preferring to go into public toilets in little villages and nicking the giant rolls they provided. He would happily boast to everyone who would listen that he hadn't bought toilet paper for years, as if he believed that anyone who did so was a fool. Although he did buy the Jaguar at one stage, most of the time he didn't have a car and he would get friends to drive him around. He loved to go out poaching, shooting rabbits or pheasants or whatever, because it meant free food and at the same time it fed his illusion that he was above the normal petty rules that everyone else lived by. He liked guns too, owning little rifles that he would fire out the kitchen window at passing birds. He often hit them because he was a good shot and he taught me how to do it too. I loved it when he taught me how to do relatively normal things, like a real parent should, rather than teaching me how to steal and cheat and eventually sell myself on the streets.

He may have rejected society's rules but he did have his own code of morality. He would never pinch money out of someone's purse, for instance; that would have seemed dishonest to him, although he had always been happy to take every penny Mum earned on the streets straight out of her hands, seeing it as his as much as hers.

Sometimes when he had company in the evenings Dad would send Terry and me upstairs to bed, but at others he liked us to stay up and be with the party till one or two in the morning, especially me. He would force me to drink whisky, watered down with orange, even though the sour taste made me gag to start with until my system grew used to it. Terry and I always preferred to be sent to bed so we could get some sleep because we wanted to go to school the following day, but there was no point arguing with him once he'd made up his mind he wanted us downstairs with him.

On other nights the exact opposite would happen and he would want to be rid of us as early as possible. If he had banished us to bed for some reason then we weren't allowed downstairs under any conditions at all and sometimes that could happen as early as four in the afternoon. As the only toilet was downstairs out the back we nearly always needed to relieve ourselves at some stage during the evening. Since the idea of defying him was unthinkable, we just had to find a way to do it upstairs, but we never had the nerve to pee out the window like him. Terry was OK since he could stand up and pee into the water tank in Dad's bedroom – although I dread to think where that water ended up; I suppose we were probably drinking it downstairs or washing in it. I couldn't reach the tank so I would have to pull back the carpet and relieve myself on the floorboards underneath. In the general filth and stench of our bedrooms Dad never noticed what we were being forced to do.

We didn't know what was going on downstairs once we were exiled to the bedroom, but we would hear some pretty funny noises and we knew he kept his private stash of pornographic magazines under the cushion of his chair. Since most of his friends were either alcoholics or prostitutes it isn't hard to guess what was happening.

I really liked most of the prostitutes he had as friends, because they were nearly always nice to me and Dad would behave better towards me when they were around. Maybe they could instinctively understand what lay in store for me because similar things probably happened to them when they were young.

There was one black prostitute called Gail who I thought was lovely and who was one of the few people able to really terrify Dad. Gail was great and used to get me to babysit for her when she was out working, sometimes bringing the punters back to her house while I was there. It didn't seem that unusual to me; it was the sort of thing I saw happening all the time around me. I suppose on some level I knew she was doing the same things Dad made me do with him, but I tried not to think about it too much.

Gail was hard as nails. She was sex mad and really wanted Dad. Although he loved sex and would boast that he could never resist fucking everything in sight, Gail made him uneasy. He liked to be the one in control, the one doing the seducing or the raping. He and Gail would go upstairs together at all times of the day and Terry and I would be able to hear them fighting or fucking or whatever else they were doing through the floor. I admired her for not just giving in to him like most people did. She once smacked him over the head with a pool cue in one of the pubs on the block. She was great. I admired people who had the courage to fight back, who didn't let someone like Dad bully them, and I wished I could be more like that myself.

Another of Dad's best friends was a prostitute called Lucy. I loved Lucy; she was a real little firecracker of a woman who had something of the gypsy about her. Dad always used to nag her like mad for being too skinny but she never took any offence at anything he said. I don't think there was ever anything sexual between them; they were just really good mates and she was another of the handful of women who were willing to stand up to him and argue back about things.

'Men don't like skinny women,' he'd tease her, but she wouldn't let him undermine her confidence or get to her like he got to everyone else.

She was always turning up at the house in the middle of the night covered in bruises after being beaten up by one or other of her pimps, all of whom called themselves her boyfriends. Each time it happened Dad would take her in and clean her up and Terry and I would find her asleep on the settee in the morning when we came downstairs. There was no doubting what she did for a living because she always dressed for the part in revealing tops, tight little mini skirts and high heels. She would be out on the game every night but she never seemed to have any money in her purse. I guess she just drank it and gave it away. A lot of prostitutes are like that: because the money doesn't seem respectable you end up frittering it away in ways you would never dream of doing if you'd earned it in a shop or a factory or any other decent profession – easy come, easy go. It always felt like 'dirty money' rather than something to be saved and looked after.

When Lucy was there she would constantly be sending me out to the shops to buy her a new pair of tights or hairspray or a comb or something. I loved running errands for her because she would always tell me to get myself some sweets while I was there, and I wanted to please her anyway. Even when I was too young to really understand what the word meant I knew she was a prostitute but I didn't care because I loved her for who she was. One day when I was nine I came back from the shops with some new tights she'd sent me for.

'Let Ria try those tights on,' Dad said and Lucy handed them over to me without really thinking.

Like any little girl I was eager to dress up like a grown-up and pulled them on happily, wanting to look as glamorous as Lucy always seemed to me.

'Try Lucy's shoes on,' Dad said once I'd got the tights on. I did what he told me, strutting awkwardly round the room about six inches taller than usual.

'Try Lucy's skirt on,' he said.

Lucy was obviously beginning to feel uncomfortable because she said she didn't want to play that game any more and tried to distract Dad, but I thought she was being a right spoilsport. Dad and I both begged her until she gave in and reluctantly handed over the skirt. I wriggled myself into it, pleased to see how grown-up my legs looked stretching out below it in tights and stilettos.

'She's got legs just like her mum,' Dad said approvingly as he watched my vampish little performance. That seemed to me to be a huge compliment because he was always going on about Mum's legs and what a fantastic figure she had.

'When she's old enough,' he told Lucy, 'I'm going to put her on the game. She's going to make a fortune.'

I'm sure Lucy knew all about his plans anyway

because he never made any secret of them, but she didn't like him flaunting it like that in front of me.

'She's too young for you to be dressing her up like that,' she protested.

'Put some make-up on her, then,' Dad said, ignoring her.

As I was begging her to make me look grown up too, she gave in. With a grim face she painted some eye make-up and lipstick on me and when I saw the results in the mirror I felt like the prettiest girl in the world.

'She looks silly,' Lucy said when she'd finished and I felt as though my balloon had been punctured. I thought I looked beautiful and it seemed to me that Dad did too, but I respected Lucy and I didn't want to seem silly in her eyes, so I went off quickly to change back into my normal clothes and wash my face. As I wiped off the make-up I remember thinking that although I had enjoyed dressing up I didn't want to be a prostitute, whatever it might involve, not even to please Dad.

'Lucy's going upstairs to do the business,' Dad used to say when she brought a punter back to our place, and I knew that was what prostitutes did. The business. That was how they earned money. More than that, I didn't want to think about. But I knew for certain at the age of nine that it wasn't what I wanted to do when I grew up.

Chapter Nine

toughening up

Although Mum's family lived in the same town as us, Terry and I never saw any of them after Mum left, not even our grandparents. It was as though the whole family had washed their hands of us, as if they were ashamed of what had happened and didn't want anything to do with us. None of them ever wrote to us or rang us or came round to see if we were OK. There were never any birthday or Christmas cards or presents. I'm sure Dad made it difficult for them, but I will never understand why they didn't at least try to help us. I guess it was easier for them all just to pretend that we had never existed.

In later years my mum's younger sister has tried to make up for it by inviting us to family events, but so many years have passed that Terry and I are complete outsiders in the family. Dad and Nanny were the only family we really knew through those years of our childhood apart from the cousins (Dad's sister's kids) who we sometimes played with at Nanny's. It was impossible for me not to love Dad when he was all I had, when he was the only person in the world who seemed to have stuck by us.

There were times, of course, when Dad would be in prison and Terry and I would be put into children's homes and those would have been the times when other members of our family could have come forward to help without fear of having to deal with Dad – but they never did, not even at Christmas. It seemed we were an inconvenience to everyone, always in the way, a burden on those who had to care for us. We couldn't understand; why didn't our nanny want us, or one of our uncles or aunts? It was as though we had vanished off the face of the earth as far as they were all concerned, and that hurt almost as much as Mum going in the first place. If everyone had deserted us, I reasoned, we really must be horrible children and Dad must be some sort of saint for putting up with us and sticking by us as much as he did.

'I'm the only person you can trust,' he kept saying, and I could see that he was right. 'I'm the only person who will ever love you.'

Sometimes he taught us things that he truly did believe were for our own good, even if he might have been doing it for the wrong reasons. Because he couldn't bear to see us cry he would teach Terry and me to fight back at every opportunity against everyone except him. If we came in from playing with other kids in the street or at school, snivelling because we'd been hit or picked on in some way, he would shout at us that we had to hit back and must never let the others see us cry. He drummed it into us that we had to be hard if we didn't want to be walked over by the rest of the world. I'd seen him put his own philosophy into practice often enough and although I didn't like his violence I could see that it gained him respect. No one ever dared to bully our dad.

'Don't fight like a girl,' he would tell me, 'don't scratch and slap, you need to learn to punch hard like a boy.'

Then he would punch us with all his strength to show us the right way to do it, unbothered by how much it might hurt. He was always hitting us unexpectedly, giving us 'dead' arms or legs for no reason, laughing at the looks of shock on our faces as we bit back the tears, telling us to toughen up, like that was the only reason he was doing it – for our own good.

Because I was shy in school, and always felt like an outsider anyway, I was an easy target for bullies. There was a particular gang of three girls who were always picking on me, laughing at my tatty clothes and taunting me for being dirty and smelly.

'You haven't got a mum,' they would shout into my face, 'because you're so horrible even she left you.'

I knew they were right so I didn't bother to argue, but

their comments left me feeling sick and empty inside. I kept coming home in tears but Dad would give me no sympathy, telling me it was all my own fault and that I should learn to stick up for myself. He had no time for a girl who 'blarred' (cried) all the time.

'You're a wimp,' he would tell me. 'Punch them, then they'll leave you alone. Then they'll respect you.'

Although I believed that the things the bullies were saying were the truth, it still hurt to hear them from other people, especially when they kept saying them over and over again, constantly reminding me what a useless, ugly, unlovable creature I was. I wanted it to stop; I wanted them to like me, or at least to leave me alone, but I didn't know of any other way to make that happen apart from Dad's way. I just couldn't find it in me to attack them like he was telling me. I didn't want to hurt anyone else in the ways Dad seemed to enjoy hurting us.

One day the girls were going on and on at me as usual and the tension was building inside my head, like an elastic band being wound tighter and tighter. Finally I'd had all I could cope with. Something inside me snapped and I totally lost all sense of reason and restraint. I flew at them, laying into them exactly as Dad had taught me to. I must have been a scary sight, landing punches all over the place without caring what happened to me as a result. The bullies obviously weren't expecting it because they put up no resistance and I won easily. As soon as I really laid into the ringleader the others melted away with their jaws hanging open and a crowd of onlookers gathered round, enjoying the spectacle of the worm turning. Even though I was meeting no resistance I still didn't stop punching until every ounce of my temper was finally drained away and my opponent was lying in a crumpled heap on the floor. I was euphoric when I saw what I'd done, all Dad's lessons having paid off, but I felt guilty at the same time. As the girl groggily pulled herself up and backed off I wanted to run after her to apologize and check that s he was all right, but I knew I couldn't do that if I wanted to hold on to my newly won reputation for being hard. I knew Dad would never have apologized for anything and I wanted to be as feared and respected and untouchable as him.

I couldn't wait to get home and tell Dad what had happened that day because I knew he would be pleased with me for doing what he had told me to do. I was glowing with pride at having stood up for myself. Dad seemed proud of me too when I described to him what had happened, giving a blow-by-blow description of my fabulous victory. I felt that for the first time ever I had really done the right thing and as a result I had finally succeeded in pleasing him; I was actually turning into someone who was worthy of his love. A few hours later, however, the father of the girl I had attacked so ferociously came to the door complaining that I'd beaten his daughter up. He wanted money because he said I'd broken her glasses and torn her dress.

I stood proudly beside Dad at the door, happy to have my victory confirmed like this, expecting him to lay into the father just as I had laid into the girl, just as he'd laid into that other dad when Terry got into a scrap in the street. But instead of sticking up for me he suddenly changed and started apologizing for my behaviour as if I was some sort of delinquent child who was giving him terrible problems. He was back to playing the sympathy card, pretending to be the beleaguered single dad struggling with difficult children. I wanted us to be a united force on the doorstep, sending our enemy scuttling away with his tail between his legs, but Dad had let me down.

As soon as the man left, Dad turned his anger on me and gave me a beating for causing him so much trouble. I was shocked and totally confused as his blows rained down on me. How could he have changed so quickly? Would I ever be able to do anything right? He'd always told me I should stick up for myself and now that I had he was hitting me again. When it was all over I was left sitting on the stairs wondering what I could ever do to please him.

Despite the fact that Dad had turned on me for causing him to get a visit from an irate father, I had to admit that he had been right about the need to stand up for myself against the bullies. From that day onwards everything changed for me at school. I now had respect and a 'reputation' for being hard. People who had witnessed the fight had told other people about it and the story of my awesome powers had probably grown in the retelling. All the people who had previously ignored me suddenly wanted to be my friends and no one ever picked on me again. Deep inside I still felt guilty about the damage I had inflicted on that poor girl, but I couldn't afford to let it show and I couldn't help but enjoy my change of status.

I might have taken on a new confidence on the outside, but I was still the same insecure little girl on the inside. Even though people no longer teased me, I still felt different to the other girls, as though I didn't belong there amongst them, as though I wasn't worthy. They all had mums and dads who had stuck around for them and who they knew loved them. That meant that in my eyes they were superior, even if I could punch harder than them. I found it difficult to play easily with other children, impossible to ever relax and join in any childlike fun. I was always on my guard, always expecting to be attacked, always holding myself in reserve. I thought everyone was laughing at me behind my back even if they no longer dared to do it to my face.

The problem with becoming Queen Bee was that I got noticed and other girls wanted the same respect that they saw me being given. Every so often someone would try to pick a fight with me in order to show that they were hard too. I never wanted to fight back but the other girls would always be watching to see my reaction when any challenge was made to my position. I knew that if I backed out of a fight the way I always wanted to I would immediately lose the respect I had earned and would risk being bullied again. Most of the time I was able to get away with just threatening the other girls, facing them down, and I was always relieved when my reputation did the intimidating for me and I didn't have to hit anyone.

Despite getting all this respect I still didn't feel like I was popular. I had been told so often over the years by Dad and by the school bullies that I was worthless and horrible that I completely believed it was true. It seemed the only friends I had were girls who wanted me to stick up for them against bullies, or the odd one or two who felt sorry for me because of my home life. That sort of popularity didn't help my self-esteem in the least. The teachers were often sympathetic towards me, as if they had seen some sort of promise that was as yet unfulfilled, but I never allowed myself to get close to any of them because Dad was always going on about us not accepting charity off anyone and I always suspected they were patronizing me when they tried to reach out and help. I guess I made it difficult for anyone who wanted to get close to me, always looking for ulterior motives for their behaviour, constantly on the defensive and ready to believe the worst about everyone.

Terry and I grew really close during our years together with Dad. Even though he was only a year older than me I believed he was much more mature and that he knew everything. I would follow him around relentlessly, never giving him a moment's peace, certain that he could make everything all right for us if he just chose to. He was a boy and he was older, so in my mind that made him my protector, my hero, the one with all the answers. But what could he do? He was just as much of a child as me and just as confused by everything that had happened to us. I was never much interested in the usual girly activities like playing with dolls; I just wanted to hang out with him and his friends. Whenever they came round I used to beg to be allowed to go with them.

'No you can't!' the other boys would say, horrified at the thought of having a small girl tagging along.

'If she can't come,' Terry would say, 'I'm not coming.'

It always worked because everyone liked Terry and wanted to hang out with him.

At home, I sometimes persuaded him to play shops with me and in return I'd play with his plastic cowboys and Indians, staging fake battles for hours on end, just like normal children our age.

We talked about almost everything together, sharing our fears and our puzzlement, but I never told him about

the sexual abuse when that started. Years later he admitted that he had guessed something was going on but didn't
know what to do about it. What could he have done?
He was just a boy and Dad and I were the two people
closest to him; there was nothing he could have said or
done that wouldn't have earned him a terrible beating.
He became very angry when it eventually all came out
into the open. He must have felt painfully left out and
awkward about the way Dad treated me when we were
young, perhaps without really knowing why. Dad had
always rubbed it in about him being Mum's favourite
and if he realized that Dad and I had secrets from him it
can only have increased his own feeling of isolation.
There was nothing I could have said to make him feel
better without actually telling him what was going on,
which would have been unbearably embarrassing for
both of us.

But I thank my lucky stars that I had Terry on my side
in those days. To have had to cope with Dad's behaviour
on my own would have been unbearable. I don't think I
would have survived.

It was always impossible to predict when some seemingly routine part of our day would erupt into a nightmare. One night when I was nine, for instance, Dad sent
me out to get him some butter. It was already getting
dark. Once I was in the shop I picked up our normal
brand of margarine without thinking, even though he

had specifically asked for butter. When I got home and he saw what I had done he exploded at me.

'You are fucking useless,' he screamed, his face only inches from mine. 'You can't do anything right!'

He ordered me to go back to the shop, which I did, keen to get out of the house again before his temper spilled into physical violence. With my heart in my mouth I bought what I thought was the right thing and hurried home again, trembling at the thought that I might still have got it wrong. Of course it turned out I had got it wrong, although even to this day I don't know what I did. He shouted and screamed again and then kicked me out of the house, issuing the usual threat: 'Don't come back till you've got it right.'

With all the trips back and forth it had grown late and by the time I got back into town the shop was closed but I was too terrified to return empty-handed. I started to walk towards home but I couldn't face the thought of the beating I was going to get for disobeying him. I knew from experience that if he had set his mind on having something specific nothing else would satisfy him, just like the brands of whisky that he always insisted on. He had told me not to go back without the right kind of butter and I couldn't disobey him, but I didn't know where else to go. I was well aware that I wouldn't get a welcome from Nanny and there wasn't anyone else to turn to.

I remembered that there was a place at the back of the

greengrocer's shop at the bottom of our road, where they dumped all the old crates and boxes to be taken away in the morning, so I decided to stay there for the night and try my luck again when the shops opened in the morning, by which time Dad would hopefully have sobered up and calmed down, or would have gone back down to the pub.

It was pitch black in the alley, away from the streetlights, and bitterly cold. I felt as though I had suddenly become homeless as I groped my way in amongst the boxes, trying to make myself a nest without being able to see what I was doing. I eventually managed to get myself into a position where I thought I would be able to sleep, but it wasn't possible. When I closed my eyes I was painfully aware of the cold and the uncomfortable corners of the boxes, and every sound from the surrounding streets seemed threatening. For the first time in my life I truly wanted to die. I wanted to be able to close my eyes and just drift away from the world, never to have to wake up and start another day of struggling.

'That'll show them,' I thought. 'Then they'll be sorry.'

I wondered if either Mum or Dad would actually feel guilty about my death and decided they almost certainly wouldn't. Dad would just have said it was all Mum's fault for leaving me as a child and she would have thought it was his fault for whatever he was doing to me after she left. Sometimes I wondered if they had the remotest idea what they were doing to any of their children with the way they behaved, or if they cared at all. I felt I must be the worst little girl on the planet; that there must be something really wrong with me that I had ended up in such a terrible situation. It was a feeling I was to become very familiar with over the years. I didn't cry as I nested amongst the old fruit boxes, because Dad had taught me how to control my tears, so I just lay there, dry eyed and miserable, staring out into the blackness of the back street wishing that my heart would stop beating and my life would end.

Eventually I became so cold, uncomfortable and scared it seemed like a better option to go home and face Dad's wrath than to stay where I was. If I couldn't will myself to die then I was going to have to get on with facing the music. I hurried back through the dark, threatening streets and was horrified when I turned the final corner to see a police car parked outside our house. I don't know exactly how long I had been gone, but it had been long enough for Dad to call the police and tell them I was missing. There were social workers as well as police in the house as I came in the front door and they were all listening to Dad playing the part of the hard-done-by father with the problem daughter, who had been abandoned by his heartless wife. Of course he hadn't thought to mention the fact that it was him who had kicked me out of the house in the first place, telling me not to come back without the right butter. I realized then that I had created even more trouble by staying away, causing all these people inconvenience and making them angry with me. I certainly wasn't going to speak up against Dad and risk making everything worse, so I hung my head in silence and probably gave the impression that I didn't give a damn about anything. If I had told them he had ordered me not to come back he would have dismissed it as a joke and made out that I was stupid for not realizing it, so there was no point in saying anything to anyone.

In the course of looking for me the police had rung my grandparents and asked for Mum's telephone number to see if she knew where I was. I suppose they thought I might have gone looking for her. They had even been talking about broadcasting my disappearance on the local news. Everyone was really angry with me when they realized I hadn't been abducted and had stayed out voluntarily, wasting their time, and I could hardly blame them since they had no idea what our lives with Dad were really like.

'Your poor dad,' someone said, 'trying to bring you up on his own, and this is how you behave, causing him all this worry.'

They all felt sorry for him, just like the old ladies who fell under his spell in the pubs, and Dad milked it for all it was worth. There was nothing I could say in my defence without telling them that I was out on the streets at that time of night because he had sent me, and I could never have brought myself to betray him like that.

After the police left, I thought I would get a beating from him for causing all that trouble, but not another word was said. He just carried on as if nothing had happened. Maybe he had genuinely been worried about me but more likely he was worried about the trouble he'd get into if something had happened to me. I expect he was grateful that I didn't tell the police why I had been out in the dark, but he had told me often enough that if anyone found out about the things he got up to he would be sent to prison again, which was an even more terrifying prospect than doing his bidding and facing the anger of the police. We already knew that when he went to prison we had no one else to turn to apart from the social services. He was all the family we had left so there was never any option but to go into care of some sort, which was like a giant leap into the unknown each time it happened. Dad was continually telling us the most terrible horror stories about foster homes and children's homes and how we could be beaten up and raped if we went there, but even without that to worry about I still would never have betrayed him, just because he was my dad and I loved him. In the great game of life Dad held all the cards.

Chapter Ten

fostering and children's homes

Dad always seemed to be battling against his depression. He would say it was because Mum had broken his heart by leaving, but he was already making suicide attempts before she finally went. When he was drunk he would often say he was going to kill himself, which made Terry and me constantly frightened that he would carry out his threats and we would come home from school one day to find him lying dead on the floor. Over the years, however, we heard him say it so frequently that we began to take less notice, until one day when I was nine he came into the house with a bottle of weed-killer and announced that he was planning to kill himself with it that afternoon. Apparently he'd read a story in the *News of the World* about a bloke who had done exactly that and now he planned to end his own life the same way. He flamboyantly opened the bottle and drank it down in front of us. Neither of us had the nerve to try and stop him. He said goodbye and went upstairs to die.

'Don't phone anybody,' was his last instruction as he left the room.

Terry and I sat staring at one another in shock. There was part of me that was thinking, 'Don't do anything, just let him go, your life would be so much easier without him,' but another part of me couldn't do that. Whatever he was like he was still our father and he was still the only relative we really had left in the world who cared anything for us at all. But did we have the nerve to disobey his direct instruction not to call anyone? Dad was always telling us never to talk to anyone about anything private that happened in our family. He would warn that they would think he couldn't cope with bringing us up and they would send us away to children's homes. If that happened, he said, we might never see him again. Sometimes we had to go into children's homes anyway because he would get caught for something and sent to prison and I would be desperate each time in case they refused to let us go back to him. If he killed himself the authorities would have no option but to farm us out to whoever they chose and there would be no going back and no one left who would give a damn what happened to us; we would be orphans.

After a few moments of waiting our nerve broke, we

decided we were going to have to risk disobeying his
orders and we rang the doctor. We explained breathlessly
what had happened and a few minutes later there was
someone knocking at the door. When we let him in the
doctor went straight upstairs to give Dad an injection and
the next thing we knew Dad was leaning out of the
bedroom window throwing up, his vomit cascading past
the front room window below. The doctor then came
back downstairs.

'He'll be all right now,' he said as he left us on our own
again. The only sounds in the house once the front door
had slammed shut were the moans and retching noises
coming from the bedroom. Looking back, I wonder what
it was that Dad had drunk. If it really had been weed-
killer, surely it would have burned his throat as he drank
it and caused him to collapse on the spot in agony? Had
he substituted something else in the bottle? Was that why
the doctor didn't have to get him to hospital? I've got no
way of finding out now.

That was the last we heard of the incident. The social
services department did not check that we were all right
or talk to us about what had happened. The good thing
was that Dad never got angry with us for disobeying him
and making that phone call, so I guess that was what he
had wanted us to do all along.

My feelings and fears after that incident were even
more mixed up and confusing. Now I felt I had to work

harder to make Dad happy so he wouldn't attempt to kill himself again. I had to try to help him to mend his broken heart, but at the same time I hated the way he treated us. I was exhausted from always being afraid and always feeling guilty.

The social workers who did come to see us from time to time continued trying to ask us questions, probably well aware that there was more going on in the family than I was letting on, and eventually when I was about ten I found the courage to emerge from my silence and confessed that Dad regularly sent us out stealing whisky and that I didn't want to do it any more. It has all become a bit of a haze in my memory but when they found that out they took us away from him and put us into a children's home called The Durdans, which as usual didn't seem to be nearly as bad as the pictures Dad had been conjuring up for us. In fact in many ways it was quite nice. The staff did their best to be kind to us and we were sent each day to a little school nearby which I absolutely loved. They bought us new clothes and gave us clean socks and underwear every day so we didn't have to wear the same filthy rags all the time, and the food was a lot better than anything we would ever get at home. But despite all these things, I still wanted to be back eating egg and chips with Dad, the one person who I believed loved me.

Dad had taken up with a new girlfriend called Kathy, who he brought in to visit us at The Durdans. I never

worried when he had new girlfriends because I was confident I was so special to him nothing would ever change
his feelings towards me. I knew he was the only one who
loved me and that he would never abandon me unless he
was forced to because he had told me so, many times. I
understood that he needed a woman in his life and I
couldn't fill that space; and nor did I want to. On top of
that I wanted a new mum and I knew Terry needed one
too.

Kathy was a lovely woman, dark and pretty, with
kind, smiley eyes. She was a genuine sweetheart with two
children of her own, both slightly older than us, and she
said what she wanted was for us all to be living together as
one big happy family. Dad had worked his magic on her
and she was as much in love with him as everyone else
seemed to be, and he was promising that as soon as he and
Kathy were sorted out he would be getting Chris and
Glen home too. He was still such a hero to me. As far as I
was concerned it wasn't his fault he drank so much, it was
Mum's, so the sooner he was able to meet someone else
and forget about her the better.

The moment I met Kathy I really wanted to be a part
of their family unit. I resolved to be a good little girl so she
would never have a reason to leave us because of my
behaviour the way that Mum had. I also knew that if
Kathy was in the house Dad would be less likely to interfere with me, trying to put his thing inside me all the

time, and I would be able to go back to just being his daughter. I yearned for that.

I'd had my long hair cut off a few days before that visit to The Durdans and Dad walked straight past at first without recognizing me, which really hurt my feelings. When he spotted me and realized what I'd done he was furious because he said he had always loved my hair. It was as if I had wilfully damaged one of his personal possessions by allowing them to cut it. Once he got over that we started chatting quite normally, although Dad always seemed to be on his guard when there were other people with us.

'Do you want to come home?' he asked in a moment when the staff had gone out of the room to make a cup of tea.

'Yeah.' I nodded enthusiastically.

'Well, tell them you lied about me sending you out to steal the whisky,' he said.

So as usual, despite the fact that lying made me feel sick with apprehension and guilt, I did exactly what he told me. I confessed to the staff that I had made up the story about the shoplifting. Even though I had already been in the home for months by that stage, they seemed to think that that changed everything and they let Terry and me go home with Dad and Kathy there and then. I couldn't believe my luck as we walked out through the doors with all our possessions packed up. I was actually going to be part of a proper home and both Kathy and Dad wanted me to be there. I loved him more than ever. We were going to be a normal family at last.

One huge advantage of having Kathy around the house was that Dad had to leave me alone sexually. It wasn't all sweetness and harmony though. Sometimes she would stand up to his bullying ways, which meant they were often rowing and separating and whenever that happened he would go back to mentally, physically and sexually abusing me again. He always had to have someone weaker than himself to pick on when his mood grew black, and he always had to have someone to relieve his sexual frustrations for him. I came to look on Kathy as my saviour and hated it whenever they fell out, frightened she would leave him for good one day and I would be at his mercy again full time.

Although we were a bit like one big family, Kathy was wise enough not to give up her house even at the times when their relationship was going well. It wasn't far from ours so we were always back and forth between the two but it meant that Dad could never completely dominate her because she had somewhere to escape to, something that Mum never had once she'd married him. Kathy adored Dad so much she actually did want to marry him and do the whole thing properly but Dad held back from that final commitment for some reason. Maybe he thought that gave him at least some power over her, or maybe he really did think Mum had been the only wife for him. Either way it was a mistake from his point of view and it was Kathy's saving.

Dad was still thieving and fighting and soon he was taken back into prison again. Kathy wasn't able to have us to stay at her place, with her own kids to look after, so the authorities put us with a foster family called the Leggetts. They already had six boys living with them and told me excitedly that they were looking forward to having a girl at last. When I got there I was thrilled to find they had even prepared me a pink girl's bedroom, but I soon realized there was going to be a price to pay for being a different gender. The boys expected me to do far more than my share of the chores, just because I was a girl. I was soon feeling that I was being really picked on, just as I had in the foster home where they called me 'dummy'. I felt they were sniggering and laughing at me behind my back all the time, although looking back now I'm not sure if they were. One day I was clearing the table after a meal and I wiped a plate into the bin using my hand instead of a knife or fork. The other children laughed at me and called me names. To them it was probably good-natured teasing, but to me it was more evidence that I was inferior to everyone I came across.

If you were in care you were given a set amount of pocket money each week. I discovered that one of the boys in the family who was younger than me was being given more money.

'Why's that?' I asked, puzzled.

'Because I'm better than you,' he replied casually and I believed him because I always believed that everyone was better than me. I remember feeling so devastated by that simple remark that that night I prayed really hard, asking God to let me go back to my daddy.

As soon as he came out of prison Dad would phone whatever home I might be in, telling me to run away and go back to him, which I always did at the first opportunity. None of the places they put me in ever felt as though they were my real home so it always seemed like the right thing to do. Although I was frightened of Dad and hated the things he did to me, he was still my dad and I still wanted to be with him. Every time I went back to him I always hoped that this time things would be different, this time he would be kind to me and he would stop doing the things I hated so much. But leopards don't change their spots.

It was like a game to him. He wanted to be able to show the social workers who were trying to do their best by me that all their efforts were feeble beside the power he had over me himself. Whatever efforts they went to in order to get me to safety he just had to snap his fingers and I would go running back to him.

When Dad got caught doing something else, probably shoplifting, he was sent back to prison. No one could really explain to us what was happening; all Terry and I knew was that the social services took us back to The Durdans for another long stay. It's hard to remember exactly how long we were there because time is so deceptive when you're young but it could have been nearly a year and I got quite settled into the local school again.

I was still convinced that I wasn't good enough for anything, just as Dad was always telling me. I remember the school used to have little maths tests each week and if I scored nine out of ten I would be eaten up inside with anger at myself for dropping one point, for not being perfect. Even if I got full marks I would tell myself it was only because the teacher had made the test especially easy that week. I found it impossible to think that I could actually be good at anything, actually be worth anything to anyone.

While I was in The Durdans a few of the girls and I would play dressing-up games and would hold beauty contests. If I won I was convinced the others had let me because they felt sorry for me and believed that I would be devastated if I lost. It didn't matter what anyone said – I was certain that I was fat and ugly and useless, having had it drilled into me for so many years. I was forever throwing myself onto my bed in fits of hysteria, although there would never be any actual tears, just a lot of shout-ing about how I loathed myself and how I wanted to end it all. If the staff heard me and asked me what was wrong I would immediately clam up and say nothing.

There was so much going on in my head at that time, so much that I was unable to explain to myself let alone anyone else. I'd never been able to express myself or communicate with anyone well anyway, whether they were family or not. Dad had never encouraged us to talk about ourselves or express our feelings; in fact he couldn't have been less interested if he'd tried. I was desperate for attention but completely unable to think of a way to let people know what I needed. It was like there was a glass wall between me and the rest of the world. I couldn't make myself heard through it and the people on the other side who wanted to help couldn't reach me.

When a lad called Harry, who was a couple of years younger than me, had a real explosion of temper and smashed everything in his room at The Durdans I watched with interest as the staff all rushed around taking notice of him, trying to find out what was behind the outburst and consoling him. Harry must have been feeling really upset to do that, I thought. Hang on a minute; I'm upset too. Harry's approach suddenly seemed like a good idea. If I had a real froth-out like Harry maybe someone would take a bit of notice of me.

I waited a couple of days to let things settle and then did exactly what I had seen him doing, smashing my room to pieces, but for some reason I didn't seem to get the same sympathetic response as Harry. They must have known that I had done it on purpose because everyone was furious with me – but at least they knew that I was seriously upset about something. I was now getting a reputation for being difficult.

A couple of times when I was a kid, probably when I was eleven and twelve, the authorities sent me on riding holidays. I got to stay in dormitories at a riding stables with other girls I had never met before and who knew nothing about me. We were each designated a horse that we would look after and ride for the week. They were the happiest times of my entire childhood. I had never ridden before but I took to it immediately, going on picnics, galloping along beaches and taking the horses swimming in the sea, which was the most wonderful feeling ever. I even won a rosette at the end of each week. I'd never won anything before in my life and I thought I was going to burst with pride and excitement. The people at the stables treated me just like everyone else, as though I was as good as them.

I remember falling in love with the first horse, a gentle grey called Shandy, and just sitting in the stables talking to him, telling him how great he was and how much I loved him. The second time I had a stubborn little brown pony called Nero but I fell in love all over again. I learnt so much in those weeks. Horses were the only things I ever learnt how to draw and we used to have bonfires in the evening and sit round them in the dark eating baked potatoes, talking and laughing. I'd never experienced anything like it. Despite being so happy on those holidays I knew they weren't reality for me and that at the end of the week I would be taken back to my old life. It never entered my head that I could actually have a life like the people who lived and worked at those stables. I wasn't good enough for that. I didn't deserve it. I could hardly understand how I had got away with being allowed to even glimpse into such a wonderful world.

I went on another group holiday to a big house where we were taught how to do various arts and crafts and outward-bound activities like canoeing. I was good at that sort of thing, particularly the sport. At one home I became obsessed with tennis, playing it every moment I could manage to get a court. I was a strong swimmer too. The very nice woman who taught swimming wanted to put me up into the higher group but I kept refusing. I liked being the best swimmer in the lower group and I didn't want to become one of the least good in the upper group. It felt so nice to actually be one of the best at something.

Dad never encouraged any of the things I was good at – the tennis, swimming or horse riding – and I was never allowed to go to after-school activities once I was back home with him again. I remember I had a bike at one stage and was very proud when I taught myself to ride it, then I got home from school one day to find out that Dad had sold it.

Maybe if I had been allowed to gain confidence and realize that I wasn't as useless as I thought, I would have had more ability to stand up for myself later and refuse to go out on the streets. But I really thought I was worthless. Dad had told me so, over and over again, so I reasoned that it had to be true.

Chapter Eleven

hockey sticks and playing hooky

Not knowing what else to do with Terry and me, the social services eventually decided to send us to a boarding school called Wymondham College. I was eleven, and it was my first year of secondary school. All our lives we had felt different and outside the norm wherever we went, whether it was within our own family, in the local schools we had been sent to or the foster and care homes. In this posh boarding school full of middle-class children, many of whose families were serving overseas in the armed forces, we stuck out like really sore thumbs. The authorities' argument for sending us there was that they wanted to get us away from Dad's influence, which was entirely understandable, but during the weekends and holidays they would send us straight back to him, so we were still completely under his influence and remained resentful and cynical about everything the staff might be trying to do for us at Wymondham.

At the introduction talk held when we first arrived at the school a teacher asked all the new pupils if we had names we preferred to be called, like Kate or Katy or Kathy if we'd been christened Katherine. For some unknown reason I piped up and said that I would prefer to be called Diane. I have no idea why I picked that name out of the air; I just didn't want to be Maria any more and I said the first name that came into my head. From then on I was known as 'Di', like I had invented a whole new identity. Except of course I hadn't; it was still the same damaged, confused and insecure me trying to fit in to yet another alien world.

In many ways sending us there was a good idea. The school regime provided an incredibly strict and structured environment, totally different to anything we had ever encountered before. Every minute of the day was account-ed for so there wasn't much time for sitting around brood-ing on the unfairness of life or on how much I was missing Dad. There were organized sports during our free time and I learnt to love games like hockey and netball, which I would never have come across otherwise. Social services had even equipped me with my own hockey stick. It felt so good to have a possession of my very own, something I dare say all the other girls there took totally for granted.

There were letter writing and reading times and chapel times, and even some weekends were filled with activities, so we were never given a chance to become bored or get up to any mischief. Once I had got over the strangeness of it all, there was a part of me that liked it, but there was no way I was ever going to feel that I fitted in with the other girls. They were all very kind and polite to me, but they were so well spoken and well travelled and lived completely different lives to anything I had ever experienced that it was a struggle to find things in common.

When you get twelve girls together in a dormitory, at the end of a day they are bound to talk about their lives outside the walls of the school. I didn't pretend to be anything I wasn't, or make any secret of the sort of background I came from, although I didn't go into too much detail of the things my dad got up to with me, but I was still able to find plenty of stories to amaze them about shoplifting and prostitutes and alcoholics. I've never been good at lying. If someone asks me a straight question I feel obliged to give them a straight answer, which was one of the reasons I hated being implicated in all Dad's various lies and scams. But I don't think the other girls always believed me, thinking I was just making stuff up for attention, or at least exaggerating the truth for dramatic effect. My home life must have seemed even more of an alien landscape to them than theirs did to me. Having been in some nice foster homes, and having been on the riding holidays, I had a bit of an idea what their lives must be like, but they would never have sat up all night drinking and playing cards with men like my dad or seen prostitutes going in and out of their house 'doing the business'. Most of them wouldn't even have been inside a council house. Prostitution was still a subject veiled in mystery for respectable people in those days, hardly even talked about in polite society. No one had made any of the explicit television series about life on the streets that were to come later.

At school I was always desperate to have a boyfriend of my own. It wasn't that I wanted any sexual contact because by then I hated all that stuff, always finding it painful, but I wanted to be part of a couple, to have someone to care for me and love me. I wanted so badly to prove Dad wrong and show him that he wasn't the only person who would ever love me that I was constantly chasing one poor boy or another, trying to make them admit that they loved me. Of course the boys I flirted with were keen to get their hands inside my bra or my knickers and when they did I would respond by becoming indignant.

'Is that all you want me for?' I would complain.

It was beginning to seem to me as if sex was all any man or boy ever wanted from any girl, but despite the mounting evidence I remained optimistic, starting again on my search after each disappointment, determined to find true platonic love somewhere. Every time I got a boy to declare his love for me I would be over the moon, certain I'd proved Dad wrong and that I wasn't the ugly unlovable creature he had always said I was. As soon as that boy chucked me because I wouldn't let him paw me I would be weeping and wailing and throwing myself down on my bed in despair, certain once more that Dad had been right after all and no one but him would ever love me.

It was during that first year at Wymondham that I started my periods. I was overjoyed when I discovered it had happened because I thought that it would mean Dad would stop having sex with me for fear that I would fall pregnant. After all, he hadn't put Mum on the game until she was safely on the Pill, so hopefully he would give me a rest from all that for a bit. I phoned him up from school to tell him the news. He was delighted to hear that I had become a woman, even though I was only eleven, but it turned out it wasn't going to make the slightest bit of difference to the way he would be treating me. The next time I went home the abuse started up again, just as always.

Even though I loved Kathy, and wanted her to be around all the time, I still felt like an outsider in the family when we were with her kids, and Dad did nothing to make it any better for me. One year we were actually all together for Christmas Day. Dad was out of prison and

Terry and I were home from school, and we were able to spend it like virtually every other family in the country. I was looking forward to it because I could remember all the Christmases he had put on for us when we were little, plucking the turkeys and all the rest, so I knew he would almost certainly be in a good mood. Kathy had made the house look really festive and we were all in the front room on the day handing round presents from under the tree. I watched as Kathy and Dad gave Kathy's daughter a box, which turned out to be filled with loads of little perfumes, all beautifully packaged. Then they gave each other gifts and as it gradually dawned on me that everyone else had something except me a pain began to grow inside my chest. I forced myself to smile and hold in the tears as I watched all the parcels being handed round and prayed I was mistaken, but still nothing came to me. Dad must have noticed my fixed expression because he laughed and chucked a packet of Maltesers into my lap.

'There you are,' he joked, 'that'll do for you.'

The most hurtful thing was that he thought it was funny to humiliate me in front of the others. He actually enjoyed reinforcing the idea that I was just a piece of shit, not worth any kindness or consideration, not deserving of anything nice, even on Christmas Day. I understood that he needed to save his money for drink so I never asked for new things, but that didn't mean I didn't want them, especially if everyone else had them. I wouldn't have wanted anything expensive, just something thoughtful and nicely wrapped to show that someone had put some time into it.

I'm not sure why Kathy hadn't got a present for me, but perhaps she hadn't been expecting me that day. It could be that she thought I was staying in school, or maybe Dad had assured her he'd got me something; I just don't remember. She was always kind to me so I know she wouldn't have left me out deliberately.

I tried to get on with Kathy's children whenever we were together, but they were older than Terry and me, too old to play with us. We never fell out or anything, but I always felt they were better than me and that I was an intruder in their family, just as I had been an intruder in the foster families we'd been farmed out to and with my own cousins when I was with them at Nanny's. There didn't seem to be anywhere in the world where I truly belonged except when it was just Dad and Terry and me.

In the end Dad even recruited Kathy in his pursuit of easy money earned at other people's expense. I would never have believed it possible, and I still find it hard to understand even today, but somehow he persuaded her to go on the game for him in exactly the same way he had persuaded Mum. She was the nicest, most intelligent, clean, beautiful woman I had ever met but still he managed it somehow. I know she put up a struggle but he literally beat her into submission. He even killed her cat in his campaign to intimidate her, swinging it by the tail and smashing its head against the wall. It was as though he could put some sort of spell on people like Kathy and me and eventually break us down and make us do whatever he wanted. If he could force strong, grown women like Mum and Kathy to do these terrible things, what chance did I have of avoiding the fate he had planned for me down on the block when I was no more than a child, a child who was still besotted with her daddy?

Chapter Twelve

the block

Dad's attitude towards me seemed to be changing as I matured, becoming more sinister and suggestive. He was beginning to see me more as a grown woman than as a child. It was as if I was part of some fantasy life he was living in his head, part of some plan that he was brooding over. Once when I was twelve, we were back home from school and we were invited to a party with him and Kathy. Dad insisted on dressing me up like a tart in a tight red dress that belonged to Kathy's daughter and talked me into getting all done up, my face painted with make-up and my hair done in an adult style, behaving like he had the time he persuaded Lucy to dress me up when I was nine.

To begin with I was excited to see how grown-up I looked, but then I started to feel less comfortable about it. I tried to back away a bit but he insisted I kept the dress and make-up on, saying he wanted to make me look eighteen for the evening. It wasn't that difficult to make me look how he wanted. I was quite mature for my age and had developed boobs before any of my mates did. In the right dress I more than looked the part.

When we got to the party Dad started acting even more strangely, more like he was my boyfriend than my father, all mauling hands, leering looks and suggestive comments. It creeped me out but I couldn't say anything without risking sending him off into a rage in front of everyone else so I just grinned, kept my eyes on the floor and put up with the embarrassment. There had been times before when he had done or said things that didn't seem appropriate between a father and daughter, apart from the obvious abuse of course, but this seemed more threatening somehow because there were other people around and he didn't seem to care if they saw or what they thought. It was as though he was flaunting me in front of everyone. He'd given me a birthday card on my twelfth birthday and I was so thrilled that he had remembered – I'd never had a card from him before. But the message written inside it was for 'my darling Maria', which sounded more like it was from a lover than a father and made me feel sick without really knowing why. This performance gave me the same feeling.

The day after the party he was still acting weird and he announced he wanted to take me to show me something.

I dutifully trotted off behind him, as I always did, happy that he was actually talking to me and being a bit like a proper father. I suppose I hoped he was going to show me something that I would enjoy, like a funfair, or that he was going to take me to the shops and buy me something nice. It was hard to stay optimistic after so many years but I kept trying. As he led me up towards the block where all the prostitutes worked my heart began to sink. I didn't know exactly what he was showing me, but I knew it was something to do with his grown-up interests rather than my childish ones and something to do with sex.

The main street on the block is called Ber Street, which is just outside the central shopping area of Norwich. That was where the better class of streetwalkers plied their trade. Further on was King Street, the haunt of girls who might have drug problems or be from out of town, having come from Ipswich or somewhere similar and been unable to get a pitch in Ber Street without being set upon by the local girls.

He proudly told me this was where Mum and Lucy and Gail and the others had worked and that he wanted to show me what I would be doing when I was ready to start work. There were a couple of pubs on the block where the girls and their pimps all used to drink in those days and where Dad was a well-known local figure. Most kids get to visit their father's offices, shops or factories, or get to admire their computers or company cars, but

Ber Street was Dad's little kingdom and he laid it before me like it was some wonderful prize, as if I would be excited at the thought of being able to work there myself one day soon.

Some of the girls were out looking for business when we got there, loitering around waiting for customers. They all seemed to know Dad and chatted to him as he went past. No doubt they were eyeing me up as a potential competitor. There was a real camaraderie amongst them all, but that didn't surprise me because I'd already experienced it at home with girls like the scary Gail and the wonderful Lucy.

Three years earlier, when Dad had made Lucy dress me up, I had decided I didn't want to be prostitute, not even to please Dad, and by the time he took me out to show me the block I was even more certain it wasn't where I wanted to end up. It all seemed sordid and frightening, even with Dad there to protect me, but I wasn't brave enough to say anything. If I had suggested I wasn't going to go along with his plan he would either have become angry and given me a beating or he would have laughed at me for being so stupid and babyish, or he would simply have ignored me and talked over my protests as if I wasn't there. Maybe if I had gone to the social services at that stage and told them exactly what he had planned for me they would have removed me there and then. But I didn't want to be removed from my family home any more than I wanted to be made to work on the streets. I wanted to be with Dad and Kathy and Terry, so I kept quiet and just hoped that he would change his mind about sending me up the block.

Kathy was the first person that I told about what Dad was doing to me whenever he had the chance and it was her who informed on him to the social services, despite her own fear of him. Even if she hadn't drawn the line at going on the street herself for him, she knew he had overstepped the mark with me. It was also her who told the authorities that Dad had taken me up to the block and shown me around, preparing me for the day when he would put me to work. If they had checked back through their files they might have found the warnings that Mum had given them when she finally left home six years before, telling them that he had been threatening to make me a prostitute since the day I was born. I dare say none of it came as a huge shock to them – everyone knew what Dad was like by then – but once Kathy had stepped forward and confirmed it all to them I suppose they were forced to take it more seriously and be seen to be doing something about it.

The day I told her the truth I had actually gone to see her in order to beg her to go back to him, because as long as she was around he would leave me alone. I had come back from school on a weekend to find they had split up yet again and I was terrified of staying at home with him on my own. As we sat together in her house she was try-ing to explain to me all the reasons why she had to break up with him: the beatings, forcing her onto the game, the heavy drinking and the bad effects he had on her chil-dren. It was all perfectly understandable from her point of view and I admired her for having the courage to leave him, but I still kept begging her to rethink her decision. My distress must have shown because eventually she asked me why I was so desperate for her to comé back. I was still terrified of betraying him and I really didn't want him to go back into prison on my account, but in the end I blurted it out. Eventually I suspect every secret grows too heavy and becomes just too painful to be con-tained any longer.

Shocked and angry, she phoned social services and they immediately moved into action. Even though she knew Dad well and had witnessed many of his depravi-ties, Kathy was still horrified by what I was telling her and immediately agreed that I should stay with her that night rather than go home to him. I felt scared, knowing that I had now put my life in someone else's hands, believ-ing that if Dad found out I had betrayed him he would kill me, and maybe he'd kill Kathy as well when he real-ized she had shopped him to the authorities. I was desper-ately anxious about what the authorities might decide to do; I didn't want anyone to stop me seeing Dad – I just wanted him to stop forcing me to have sex with him. All weekend I felt panicky and scared and nothing Kathy could say or do would calm me down.

After that weekend I was sent back to Wymondham without seeing Dad and the social services responded to the information Kathy had given them by coming to the school to do tests on me, wanting to gather evidence that they could use against Dad in court. The fact that they wanted to do the tests seemed to suggest they believed me, which was a relief, even though I didn't like the idea of having a doctor probing around inside me. They wanted me to tell them every detail of what had happened and then they went looking for proof to back up my story. It felt like I was losing control of my own life, handing it over to the grown-ups, but of course it was an illusion because I had never had any control really; that had always rested in Dad's hands when he was around and in the hands of social workers whenever he was taken away. All I had ever had was a horrible secret, and now I had given it away.

If I had felt different to the other girls at school before, I felt like a complete alien now that the staff were moving discreetly into action to support me. How was I going to be able to just breeze back into class after all this and mingle with everyone else as if my life was just like theirs?

I was taken to see the doctor and to my horror he announced after doing the tests that although there was evidence of sexual activity, my hymen was still intact. Despite all the pain Dad had inflicted every time he tried to enter me, he hadn't succeeded in taking my virginity. Despite trying to force himself into me he had been just too big to get very far. What horrified me the most about this news was the thought that now they might not believe me, that they would think I was making it all up just to get attention. I felt desperately let down and worried about what Dad would say when I next saw him. He would be furious that I had tried to betray him, but triumphant that I had failed to provide the evidence needed to prosecute him. It was the worst possible outcome.

Somehow Dad persuaded Kathy to go back to him even when she knew all about what he had done to me, which I found hard to understand. He then didn't bother to turn up to the next meeting with my social worker. It was as though he was showing them he didn't have to live by their small-minded rules; that he wasn't intimidated by them and all their official powers. When he did finally show up at his own convenience he vehemently denied all the allegations I'd made.

'Look how she lied about me sending her out to steal whisky,' he said. 'She's evil. I don't want her back home after this.'

He was playing some diabolical game of mental chess with me and with the rest of the world. It was him who had suggested I told them I had lied about him making me steal the whisky, and now he was using that false confession to prove that I was a liar. There was nothing I could say in my defence that wouldn't make me sound even worse.

Sometimes he seemed to be flaunting his lifestyle in the faces of the people who tried to interrogate him, as if he was trying to show them up for being petty and small minded, painting himself as some grand, bohemian libertine, unfettered by their petty rules and morals. He admitted that because he rented two of our three bedrooms out Terry and I often slept in his bed with him.

'Sometimes I might put my leg over Terry in my sleep,' he told them, 'thinking I'm with a woman.'

The social services, however, were obviously coming to the conclusion that there was no smoke without fire and even if I was still technically a virgin, it would only be a matter of time before they caught him. Dad must have realized they were closing in on him and his depression returned. After they had talked to him Kathy rang the social worker in charge of the case to tell her that Dad had become suicidal and that he had now admitted to sending us out to steal whisky for him. Maybe he thought that if he admitted to one thing then they would be more likely to believe him when he denied abusing me, or maybe he had become too depressed to even care what happened to him any more. It was a relief to know that he was admitting it was him who was the liar and not me, but I was worried that if he got too depressed he might try to kill himself again. I didn't want to be the cause of that. He was still the most important person in my life and I loved him despite everything.

By then the police were involved and I realized it was possible Dad was going to be sent to prison yet again because of me. The staff at school and social workers kept telling me I had nothing to worry about, nothing to blame myself for, but I knew they were wrong. I walked around with a huge cloud over my head, almost wishing I'd kept my mouth shut, worrying over things constantly.

The reports that teachers and social workers did about me during those years show they were almost as confused about what was going on in my head as I was. At one stage my housemistress at Wymondham wrote: 'Maria is in some ways functioning at a four- or five-year-old level and in others at a sixteen-year-old level, plus being an intelligent twelve year old.' She then made the extraordinary statement: 'Maria is over-fond of her dad and wants him close to her, up to a certain point, and beyond that she starts complaining.' Isn't that how a little girl should feel about her father? I loved my daddy; I just didn't want him doing those things to me. Was that so unreasonable?

There were all sorts of meetings to discuss whether Terry and I should be allowed home for weekends at all. At one stage my grandmother offered to have Terry at her bungalow, but she didn't offer to have me, confirming my early feelings that she'd never liked me. As far as she was concerned I was the troublemaker in the family, telling lies about her son, spreading false rumours, bringing dishonour and scandal down on all of us. She would never have been able to admit that he was capable of doing the things that I had accused him of. To complicate matters even further Dad was in the process of being evicted from his house because the council had discovered he was subletting the rooms that were meant to be for us. His angle for hanging onto the house was to say that he had to have a home for his children when we came back from school, but if we weren't allowed to see him that would undermine his argument, particularly if he was renting out the rooms.

Then in another interview he suggested I was just trying to get back at him by making up these stories because he had bought Terry a £50 watch for his birthday but hadn't bought me anything. It was certainly true that he had done that, but I was used to things like that. It always hurt but it also made me more anxious to please him, more anxious to make myself a better daughter so I would deserve to be given presents too. It certainly didn't make me want to get him sent to prison.

'And anyway,' he said right at the end of the interview, 'even if I had done these things, if she really loved her dad why would she say such a thing?'

Social services actually had his words down in writing, as if he was admitting that a child should not tell tales on her father if she loved him, no matter what he might have done to her. It seemed to me to be practically a cast-iron admission of guilt.

While all this was going on the authorities needed to find us somewhere else to go during school holidays. Break was a charity that had been started by a couple called Mr and Mrs Davison to provide respite care for disabled children. They had two houses, one called Magpie and one called Rainbow. Magpie had become a general children's home and the council decided to send Terry and me there during the holidays while we were attending Wymond-ham College so that we didn't have to go back to Dad.

I had some of my happiest times at Break, particularly when a group of us used to go down to the nearby beach where we would spend hours swimming during the summer or just walking or sitting and talking in the winter. We liked it better out of season when the holidaymakers had all gone home and we had the sands to ourselves. I used to go into the disabled house to help feed the children who lived there. I loved doing that because disabled people don't judge you; they just accept you for who you are. I never felt they were looking at me and wondering what I was doing there or thinking that I didn't belong or looking down at me. I felt by helping them I was making up a little for being such a crap person the rest of the time.

By the time Terry and I were at Break the Davisons had opened a third house and the whole operation was starting to develop into the huge charity it is today. But even though they were giving me the happiest times I had ever experienced, whenever I spoke to Dad on the phone he nagged me to run away and come back to him, and so finally I did. It might be hard to understand, but I'd missed him and I'd been so upset about betraying him and worried that he might not forgive me that I was really happy when he phoned and asked me to come home.

I was nervous about the reception I might get but he didn't seem to hold it against me that I had told Kathy about what he was doing to me, or that he might end up in prison for it. He just seemed to accept it as being part of life. I was so relieved that he still wanted to see me and felt so guilty about betraying him that I would do whatever he asked. I didn't want to accept the help that was being offered by everyone else. My opinion of myself was so low that even when people showed a genuine concern for my welfare I dismissed them as interfering busybodies who were 'just doing their jobs' – an attitude I had learnt directly from Dad.

Even at Break Terry and I were made to feel different because all the other children went to the local secondary school while we were sent off back to Wymondham College at the end of each weekend and every holiday, which meant we didn't really fit in at either place.

I must have been giving off a lot of contradictory signals to everyone because my social workers' reports at the time paint a very odd picture.

'Maria went home on 23rd December,' one wrote. 'Terry Snr phoned asking if Maria could stay for the weekend. Spoke to Maria also, she'd like to stay with Dad. Phoned Mrs Davison, she agrees with Maria staying with Dad until Sunday. They've all been staying at Kathy's house, which means the likelihood of Terry and Maria indulging in any sort of sexual activity is that much less. Whether they did in the past is debatable and it's a risk that has to be taken since Maria will never be content anywhere unless she can see her father.'

I saw it as him raping me; they saw it as the pair of us 'indulging in sexual activity'. It seemed like they thought I had as much to do with instigating it as he did. By constantly running back to him I was making it look like I was asking for it, I suppose, but that wasn't how I saw it. I might have been guilty of some poor judgements when it came to putting myself in dangerous situations with him, but he was an adult who should have known better and I was a child in need of protection. I wonder if the social worker involved would have been happy to send her own daughter home for the weekend with Dad, however much the girl might have wanted to go?

All my life Dad had drummed it into me that wherever the authorities took me I should take the first opportunity to run away and go back to him. I never really questioned that wisdom, even though I sometimes knew I was better off in the places they sent me to. He was my dad, it seemed right that I should want to be back with him, it was just the way things were. At one stage they said he could only visit me under supervision, but he wouldn't have that. He threw a tantrum and said that if he couldn't see me on his own he didn't want to see me at all. I guess he knew he could brainwash me better when he had me to himself. Another adult in the room at the same time would have been able to see through his manipulations, would have cramped his style.

I think that in a funny way I broke his heart by betraying him to Kathy and the social services because he truly believed I was his property, to do with as he pleased. It was as if he was disappointed and puzzled to think that I mightn't be going to become a successful prostitute and a credit to his teaching, able to support him for the rest of his life. Maybe he felt the same way as respectable parents feel when their children decide not to become doctors or lawyers after family hopes have been raised. Not that he allowed this setback to interrupt his plans for long.

Chapter Thirteen

the first client

I kept running back to Dad and letting him hide me from the authorities for days or weeks on end, not realizing that I was playing straight into his hands. He continued interfering with me and finally succeeded in achieving full penetration over the course of time. I couldn't pinpoint an exact occasion when I lost my virginity fully because it hurt so much every time. It was while I was with him on one of these escapes from school, when I was thirteen, that he must have decided the time was right for me to start earning him money, now that he had succeeded in breaking me in himself – and he knew just how he wanted to get me started.

He had a friend called Peter, a big, fat, smelly Irish drinking companion who spent a lot of his time working away from home, probably on the oil rigs in the North Sea. Peter always had plenty of cash in his pocket and no one to spend it on except himself, which made him a tempting target for Dad. When he and Dad were together they would always drink heavily and I dare say Peter was buying most of the rounds. One night, I had run away from school and had gone to find Dad as usual. He welcomed me back and took me out drinking with him and Peter. At that time he liked to buy me vodka and limes and none of the pubs we went to ever said anything, even though they must have known how young I was. I was used to getting drunk with Dad's friends; I'd been doing it since I was eight or nine, when I used to drink whisky and orange and play cards till all hours of the morning in our front room, so I had no reason to be particularly suspicious of their motives that day any more than any other.

At the end of the evening they wended their way back to Peter's flat with me in tow, picking up a Chinese takeaway on the way. It was a horrible, dirty, dingy flat, the sort of place you might expect to find a wino living, but I was too drunk and hungry to care much about my surroundings. Just being with my dad was enough to make me happy. I settled onto the settee and opened up the Chinese.

However many vodkas I had put down that night I was still sober enough to put up a fight when Peter started making a clumsy and unwelcome pass at me. Men had made unwelcome passes at me before and I was confident

I could keep him at bay, especially with Dad there to protect me. I'd seen Dad beat up enough people to be sure that dealing with a fat, drunk Peter wouldn't give him any trouble. I hoped Peter would take the hint and give up before Dad lost his temper and beat him to a jelly.

The next thing I knew I was grabbed, thrown off the settee amidst flying Chinese food cartons and pinned down on the floor. My head suddenly cleared with the shock and I realized Dad was holding my arms back to allow Peter to screw me. My father wasn't going to fight to protect me because he had sold me. I struggled and shouted at them both to get off me.

'Shut up!' Dad screamed, apparently furious that I was showing him up like this by making such a fuss.

There was nothing I could do against the strength and weight of two grown men and eventually I gave up even trying.

'Relax,' Dad instructed as always, 'because it's going to happen. You're not going to get away from it so just get on with it. The more you relax, the better it will be for you.'

I turned my head away so I didn't have to look at their faces as Peter did what he wanted to do and I stared hard at the overturned cartons and the spilled Chinese food on the carpet that had seemed so appetizing just a few moments earlier. All I could think was that this was all I was worth, this was what I was reduced to, lying amidst the rubbish, being used up and disposed of like the cheap spilled food on the floor. This was all my own father thought of me.

I somehow felt more violated than I ever had when Dad had done it to me himself because Peter was a virtual stranger and because he was so disgusting physically. Dad always told me he was the only one who loved me, so I could be bloody sure Peter had no feelings towards me whatsoever. He just wanted some quick relief and a bit of underage action. Because they didn't exchange any words during the whole scene I knew that they must have planned it before, that Dad had pimped me just as he had pimped Mum and Kathy and all the others. I knew Peter must have paid because I was sure Dad would never have given me to another man for free. He was always jealous of me even having a boyfriend, but somehow that didn't seem to matter when there was money to be earned. I had become just another dodgy little business transaction to him, a bit of a cash cow, and Peter was no threat to his own power or control over me.

'You shouldn't be giving it away,' were the exact words I'd heard him use to women a hundred times before, 'when you could be charging for it.'

I knew that he genuinely had difficulty understanding why every woman didn't go on the game. In some ways I think he believed most of them did, one way or another. He always said that married women who didn't work lived off their husbands and provided sexual favours in return. He didn't think that was any different to openly selling your wares to different men on the street.

Many years later, when I had been moved to another children's home, Peter used to send me money from time to time, even though I never had sex with him again after that first experience. Maybe he had a conscience after all. But Dad certainly didn't because from that night onwards he saw me as a permanent source of income and started taking me up the block to work just like Mum, leading me deep into his own personal world.

The first night I worked on the block I was on the run from Break. I think Dad had just come out of prison for something and had encouraged me to come and see him. We couldn't go to his flat to stay because that would have been the first place the authorities would have gone to look for me, so we went round to Lucy and Twiggy's place. Twiggy was Lucy's on-and-off boyfriend for years and was a lovely old boy. Even though I was scared about what Dad had planned for me that night, I felt comfortable being with them. They made it seem like it was all just a normal day's work. I drank an awful lot of vodka before we went out in order to get my courage up. Most prostitutes have to be drunk or high in order to deal with the fear of being out on the street, especially when they're starting out. Afterwards they drink more because they want to drown out the memory of what they've just done, which is why there is such a culture of alcohol and drugs around the business. I didn't know anything about drugs in those days and that was one thing Dad always said he was totally against. He thought he was too good for the dirty, scruffy hippy scene of the time.

That night Dad told me what to wear and supervised me painting my face and then he took me out to Ber Street. I just felt an overwhelming sense of hopelessness. There was no way out of it, so I might as well get it over with. I obeyed him automatically, in robot mode.

'Walk up to the car when it stops,' he instructed, 'open the passenger door and ask, "Do you want business?" If they say "Yes, how much?" you say "Seven pounds in the car or ten pounds at the house."'

He stayed in the shadows behind me, pushing me towards the cars as they slowed down, whispering encouragement as I wobbled forward on my high heels, fuelled up on vodka and lime. It was frightening, but it wasn't exactly difficult. If a car containing a single man was cruising in that area it was certain that he was looking for the one thing I was selling.

'Do you want business?' I asked the first one, terms were agreed and I got in the car and that was it. I probably managed to service four or five punters that first night. I don't have any clear memories of the men or the sex, just a sense of total revulsion. Did these men have any idea that I was only thirteen? Would it have mattered to them if they did? Surely there was no way I could pass for sixteen, even in the dark? But no one stopped and said, 'You're too young, darling,' because they all wanted a piece.

Dad had bought a bottle of whisky to take back to the house after I'd earned my money. Relieved it was all over and I had survived, I swallowed several glasses in quick succession and then threw up all over his suit trousers. The whisky probably didn't mix too well with the vodka still swilling around in my stomach from earlier, not to mention all the adrenaline that must have been coursing through my body. I thought Dad would kill me for spoiling his clothes but he didn't even get angry, just seemed to think it was funny that I had got myself into such a terrible state.

He was always good at helping people when they were drunk or ill or had been beaten up. Whenever one of his friends like Lucy turned up on the doorstep in a bad state he would always take them in and do whatever was needed. Whereas most people might think they had brought such things on themselves he would think it was perfectly understandable. Maybe he knew that at vulnerable moments like that he would be able to turn people into anything he wanted, make them prostitutes or alcoholics, make them dependent on him and grateful to him for not judging them. He liked people to think he would always be there for them, no matter how badly they behaved. If I was drunk and throwing up I was easier to manipulate and control.

'That's life,' he said cheerfully as he cleaned my vomit off his trousers.

We stayed at Lucy and Twiggy's for a few days that time but the police must have got wind of where I was because they came looking for me to take me back to the children's home. When they heard the police at the door Dad and Lucy hid me in the cupboard under the stairs. As I sat scrunched up in the dark I was hoping the police would find me and take me with them because I didn't want to go on the streets any more. I felt ready to return to the safety of the home but I wasn't going to call out and give myself away because I knew that would upset Dad. Pleasing him was always the most important thing, so I stayed silent in the darkness under the stairs, my heart thumping, watching the passing shadows through the cracks in the boards, listening as the police checked all over the house but didn't even bother to open the door I was leaning against. I listened to them finishing the search and leaving the house with mixed feelings.

From then on, I began to work on the block regularly. While I was working, Dad was completely in control of everything I did, and he loved it. Every night he would decide what I should wear and how I should paint up my face. Once he knew I had got the hang of it he would leave me out on the pavement to wait for business while he disappeared into one of the nearby pubs where he was a well-known face, popping out every so often to check on how I was getting on. He didn't need to be there much after the first few times because he had taught me exactly what to do.

Occasionally I would take men back to Dad's flat but mostly I worked in the cars. The routine was almost always the same and the whole transaction never took long because the guys had always got themselves so worked up by the time I got into the car that the actual act was all over in a few seconds. Most of the turn-on for them was the risk of coming looking for a prostitute in a dangerous area, of slowing down the car and talking to us, the buzz of the unknown. They enjoyed the thought that they were walking on the wild side of life; the side where people like me and my dad were lying in wait for them.

There was a little lane in a nice village just outside the city ring road, which was where most of the men would drive us girls once they had picked us up. It was well known for being a sort of 'lovers' lane' with cars parked up in all the little nooks and crannies as the business was done. If there were too many cars there already, or the police were parked there watching what was happening, then the punter would have to drive on and find somewhere else to do the business, like an empty multi-storey car park. They usually seemed to know where they were going, unless they were from out of town, when they would need some suggestions and directions. Most of the customers seemed the same to me. I guess they were businessmen, always clean, polite and well suited, driving posh, shiny company cars. If someone rolled up to the kerb in a battered old van looking a bit rough we would tell them to piss off and they would have to go to one of the other streets where the girls could afford to be less choosy.

The drive to the location was usually the most frightening bit of the operation, wondering if they would stop or where they would go or whether they would turn nasty when they were asked for money. Nearly all of them were fine and acted in exactly the same way but every time I got into a car with a stranger I knew I was putting my life on the line because there was always a chance that this would be the sort of madman or sadist who got his kicks from battering or strangling or stabbing girls like me.

Once the punter had found somewhere to park he would hand over the money. Then there would often be a row about condoms. Every client always wanted to do it without but I was never willing to do that. Not only did I not want to get pregnant, but I had also been living amongst prostitutes for long enough to know about the dangers of infections and sexually transmitted diseases; I'd overheard Lucy and Gail discussing it often enough.

Sometimes the guys would offer silly money, like a hundred pounds, to be allowed to do it without, but I was never tempted. Some of the more desperate girls who had drink or drug habits to finance would probably be more easily persuaded. I guess the punters are a bit more used to the idea of condoms these days, but in the late 1970s no one knew anything about Aids so there wasn't the same level of caution. I would never do blow jobs either, having hated it so much when Dad made me do it to him, so it was nearly always just straight sex that I was selling.

Once the deal was agreed and the money exchanged I would tilt the passenger seat back as far as it would go and slide my knickers off. By that time the punters would be absolutely desperate for it, and often nervous about being caught at the same time, which added still more to their fumbling haste and their level of excitement. They would struggle out of their jackets, undo their trousers and roll over between my legs. I would then stick my feet up on the dashboard and it would all be over in a matter of seconds. A few minutes later I would have wriggled back into my knickers, pulled the seat up into its normal position and we would be driving back to the block. Usually I could be out on the pavement again, re-adjusting myself and getting ready to approach my next customer, within quarter of an hour of getting into the previous car.

I was supposed to give every penny that I earned to Dad, but once he got used to me being up there he became bored and started disappearing into one or other of the pubs. He would then reappear less and less often and had less and less idea of what was actually going on. Once I was more experienced I would do a couple of punters while he was away and when he came out and asked how business was I'd tell him there hadn't been any yet, keeping the money well hidden. I had also put my basic price up to a tenner without telling him, so I could keep back some for myself.

At that time I was the youngest girl working on the block and the older women didn't like me being there, stealing their punters, but they wouldn't do anything about it because they knew Dad was around and looking after me. There were quite often fights amongst the women, especially if girls from other towns tried to muscle in. I knew that if I hadn't had Dad's protection I would have been given a hard time, but then again if it hadn't been for him I wouldn't have been there at all.

Dad gave me a little skewer attached to a ring that I wore on my finger, saying I could use it if I ever needed to defend myself. The skewer was cradled in the palm of my hand ready to swivel round onto my knuckles in a dangerous situation, but I never actually found the courage to use it. If I'd tried to use a weapon like that I think I would probably have come off worst in the encounter and I could even have ended up dead. I became more confident about the way I dealt with punters over time but I never lost that fear that the next stranger whose car I got into would be the one who murdered me.

Although I tried to pick my customers carefully it wasn't always possible to sum someone up accurately in the few seconds between opening the car door and getting in. There was one occasion when the moment I climbed into the car and closed the door behind me I had a bad feeling, even though it was still daylight, a time when everything normally felt safer. The guy at the wheel looked like one of my normal everyday punters but once we were driving he told me he didn't want to go to the lane where I usually went and drove instead to a new location in the middle of nowhere. He had taken control of the situation in a way that made me uneasy. I said nothing, already sensing that he wasn't someone to mess about with and knowing from dealing with Dad when he behaved like this that it was important not to aggravate the situation. When he eventually stopped the car and I asked for the money he brushed it aside.

'Later,' he said.

But that was a golden rule that Dad and Lucy and everyone else I knew in the business had always drummed into me. Always get the money up front. As I was beginning to feel a bit scared anyway I used his reluctance to pay as an excuse to call the deal off and fumbled to get out of the car. The moment my fingers touched the door handle he pulled me back into the seat with all his strength and smacked me hard in the mouth. I knew then not to argue or fight any more, just to give in. Years of experience with Dad and his tempers told me that this was a man who didn't care how much damage he inflicted in order to have his own way. I knew that if he was willing to act like this right from the start then he might be prepared to do far worse if I didn't cooperate. I could tell that he didn't see me as a person at all and that there would be no chance of appealing to his better nature.

I know it seems odd to claim that I was raped, given that I was selling sex, but that was how it felt. I hadn't given my consent to it and yet he did it anyway, leaving me feeling violated, cheated and furious. I said nothing – just waited for it to be over and hoped he wouldn't turn really nasty afterwards. Once he'd finished, he nicked whatever money I had in my purse before pushing me out of the car, flinging my bag out after me and driving off leaving me in a heap on the side of the road, scrabbling around on the ground for my scattered possessions, every last scrap of human dignity gone.

I was so hurt and angry I wanted to report him to the police or talk about it to someone, but what was the point? I was an underage prostitute on the run from a children's home: what chance did I have of getting any sympathy from anyone? I knew from things I'd heard the other girls saying that I was lucky to have got away as lightly as I had. In the end all I'd lost was the money and my dignity, but I could have ended up beaten to a pulp or even dead.

I was arrested a couple of times for soliciting but because I was underage I just received cautions. That was always Dad's trump card when persuading me to do anything illegal, the fact that I was too young to be prosecuted. The police were nearly always looking for me anyway because I was known to have run away from school or from some children's home or other. One time I was cautioned for carrying an offensive weapon when a policeman noticed the skewer on my ring.

Strangely enough, some of the police seemed more concerned about the worry I was causing my father than about the damage that was happening to me. One time I was picked up by a policeman on Ber Street who knew that not only was I in care and under age, but I was also a ward of court. I knew this man was a friend of Dad's. Dad had recently been beaten up for some reason, and this guy seemed to know all about it.

'You do cause your dad a lot of problems,' the policeman tutted as he drove me back to Dad's flat. He was talking about Dad as if he was a sweet old man who couldn't understand why his delinquent daughter was the way she was, rather than the man who had instigated and encouraged everything I had ever done wrong in my life. On the way there he stopped off at the fish and chip shop to get something for us to take for Dad's supper, 'to cheer him up' as he put it.

The only explanation I can think of why Dad was allowed to get away with as much as he was, was because he was a grass – but there is no way he would ever admit to such a disgraceful thing. In the sort of circles Dad moves in, pimping your underage daughter is one thing, grassing to the police quite another.

Chapter Fourteen

mum's return

Eventually the authorities at Wymondham College were forced to expel me halfway through my second year there because of the number of times I had run away. I'm sure they made allowances for my family background but in the end I understood that they had to show the other pupils that it simply wasn't acceptable to take off from school whenever you felt like it. Terry got expelled a bit later for other minor misdemeanours. Although it was a great school, it had never really been a suitable place for children with as many problems as we had.

At Break I had made a really good friend called Mel and I hoped that now Wymondham had chucked me out I would be able to go to the local school with her and another girl called Fiona, but the social workers decided I should be enrolled in yet another school – North Walsham Girls'

High – which was at least ten miles away from the home. That meant I had to get up an hour earlier than everyone else and catch a different bus on my own. I could never understand why I always had to be treated differently, kept separate from everyone as though I had some sort of infectious disease.

Mel and I had a lot in common. Her dad was friendly with my dad to start with so she understood a fair bit about the sort of world I had come from. He was another alcoholic and had been violent towards her mum, which was why she had ended up in care. Unlike the girls at Wymondham she understood a lot of what I was going through, although I thought she always seemed a real lady compared to me. I was the one who always seemed to get into trouble with the staff while Mel gave the appearance of floating above it all. Everyone at the home loved her, including me. It would be fair to say I was in awe of her. Although she was a few months older than me she was like my little sister and I felt I had to be really protective of her.

I wish now that I had felt more comfortable at Wymondham and had stayed all the way through because then I would have come out with a great education and some qualifications. I would also have been able to keep up the sports that I loved, but I didn't appreciate any of that at the time; all I knew was I felt I was the wrong person in the wrong place, somewhere I didn't fit in. Dad only had to give me the slightest encouragement to give it all up. But where was I going to fit in? On the block with him? I really didn't want to keep doing that.

After leaving Wymondham I never saw my hockey stick or tennis racket again, nor the model swan that week after week I had lovingly crafted from a block of wood in the woodwork classes and was really proud of. The fact that no one thought these were things worth keeping safe for me reinforced my own certainty that I was worthless myself.

When I started at North Walsham Girls' High at the age of thirteen I was still heavily into my tennis. One day when I was having a tennis lesson at school I started getting horrendous period pains and being sick. I was sent to the sick room and Mrs Davison was called from Break to come and collect me. I was absolutely terrified that I was going to be in trouble for having made her come to pick me up. I was so ashamed and frightened, but she couldn't have been kinder. She took me home and let me lie on the settee with a blanket over me, watching Wimbledon while the staff came back and forth with warm milky drinks and paracetamol and whatever else I needed to help me get better. These small acts of kindness always overwhelmed me and made me feel like a worthwhile human being, but never for long. I never got over the belief that they didn't really care for me, that they were only doing their job.

In all my confusion and anger and unhappiness in the months after Dad made me go on the game, I had started cutting my arms with knives and any other sharp implement I could get my hands on. I don't think I wanted to actually kill myself, although I wouldn't have cared too much if I had thought I was going to die; I just wanted to hurt myself because I thought I was so worthless I didn't deserve to be treated any better. It was like I wanted to punish myself for being such a terrible person. I suppose also that it gave me some kind of control over my body, in ways that I didn't have otherwise. When the blood started to flow, I always felt a sense of release, however momentary.

I never stopped running back to Dad but I became much more reluctant, never knowing whether he planned to put me out on the street to work, or to spend the weekend abusing me himself. One Saturday at Break I kept getting phone calls from Terry, who was back at home on a visit. At this stage Terry didn't know anything about what Dad was making me do. When I answered the phone Dad came on the line saying the two of them were off for a day out at the seaside in Yarmouth with Kathy.

'Do you want to come?' he asked.

'I can't,' I said, knowing that the staff at Break would never give me permission for a day out with Dad, even if Kathy was there.

'Just get on the train,' he said, 'and I'll meet it at Norwich and pay your fare.'

I held out for a while, making excuses, but I really wanted to go if it was just going to be a family outing, and Dad was always so persuasive when he was leading someone astray. Only when I read my social services reports many years later did I realize that the authorities at Break knew exactly what was going on that day and considered getting the police to meet me at Norwich station, before thinking better of it and deciding to let me go. I can't actually remember if we ever got to Yarmouth but I do remember Dad abusing me that weekend. I don't think Kathy had been there at all; he had just used her as bait to get me to run away.

He kept me hidden from the police that night, and the next day we went round to Nanny's for lunch. I was even quieter than usual, feeling devastated at him lying to me and using me yet again. I had sunk into a mood and it was impossible to drag myself out of it. I didn't want to be there any more, but I didn't want to be back at Break and away from what family I did have either. My cousins were at Nanny's bungalow too that Sunday and we all hung out in the next-door garage after lunch, escaping from the adults but with nothing else to do. Because of my sullen mood the atmosphere was even more awkward than usual.

I went back to Break voluntarily that night and, feeling desperate to share my unhappiness with someone,

I told my friend Mel everything that had happened, including the fact that Dad had screwed me. Although her dad was a drinker and violent he had obviously never tried anything like that on with her because she was appalled and immediately told a member of staff who contacted the police. I'm not sure if I had hoped she would do that or if I had hoped she would keep it secret; maybe a bit of both because I was totally confused about what I did want most of the time. Anyway, the police arrived at the school and said that in order to be able to prove in a court of law what Dad had done they had to get me examined within forty-eight hours so they could gather the evidence while it was still fresh.

'This time we will really be able to get him,' they assured me.

I felt torn in two. Half of me wanted to do whatever was necessary to stop Dad from abusing me, but the other half dreaded the idea of him being sent to prison and ending up hating me for betraying him yet again.

It was late and dark when they got me to the police station and they wouldn't let Mel come with me because they said she was too young. I had all the usual tests and they asked me to spit into a test tube because Dad had kissed me during the sex and would have left traces of his saliva in mine.

The stress of the following weeks made my period late so then I had to take a pregacy test. The thought that I might be pregnant by my own father was mortifying, but thankfully it proved to be a false alarm.

When he was confronted with the accusation that I had had sex with someone over that weekend while I was in his care, Dad immediately had a cover story ready.

'She must have screwed one of her cousins in the garage that Sunday afternoon,' he suggested, 'round at my mum's.'

I was furious that he would tell such a blatant lie about me just to cover his own back, making it look like I was some sort of sex maniac, desperate to go with anyone who asked. I was sure the tests would prove that what he was saying wasn't true but the results never seemed to arrive, or if they did no one seemed to think they should tell me anything about them. After months of worry the staff told me that the police were dropping the charges. Nobody ever explained to me why that had happened, but Dad told everyone that the reason they couldn't press charges was because they had found more than one man's semen inside me so I had obviously been screwing around that weekend. I was devastated that the authorities had failed me again and that Dad would be willing to say such things about me.

It was all just a game to him, like cat and mouse. He would boast that he could twist social services round his little finger and he was right. Looking back now I wonder if the police dropped the charges in exchange for some information from Dad on some other criminal, but even if that was true I know he would never admit it. Not in a million years.

One day when I was fourteen I was in the kitchen at Break leaning against the hatch to the dining room, talking to someone on the other side. The huge kettle had been filled to make hot drinks for our supper and the flames from the gas ring were licking up the side. I felt an itch on my back and looked over my shoulder to discover the blouse I was wearing, which I had borrowed from a member of staff, was in flames. I ran out screaming into the hallway, the flames streaming behind me. Another member of staff dragged me out through a door and rugby tackled me to the ground, rolling me in the snow that lay on the ground outside. I ended up in hospital for a week, lying on my front, my back covered in angry great blisters. When I came out of hospital I still had to wear padding on my back, making me even more certain I was an unattractive mess of a person. The doctors warned me that I would end up scarred but in fact it all healed eventually.

Soon after that Dad was sent to prison again for something unrelated to me. I was quite settled at Break with Terry but I was really beginning to feel the loss of having no other family apart from him and Dad. Adore Dad though I did, I had finally realized that I was never going to be able to rely on him to be there for me, and if he was there he was always going to be messing with me or forcing me to go with other men. I desperately wanted to have someone else I could rely on and it wasn't fair to put all my problems onto Terry, who had enough troubles of his own trying to cope with our family situation. Mel had eventually told him about Dad making me work on the block and he went ballistic, saying he was going to knife him. He was so upset about it that I thought it wasn't fair to put that pressure on him any more.

So I asked social services to contact Mum. With Dad out of the way I thought it would be safe for her to come and see us and I really wanted to meet her, having no memory of her from the time when she lived with us. I was trying hard not to hate her for walking out on us and I was curious to know what she was like and why she had made no effort to contact us all through those years. I thought we would have a lot in common now since Dad had treated us both in pretty much identical ways.

Social services promised they would do their best and they eventually tracked her down. She was working in a hotel in Eastbourne on the south coast and lodging in a friend's house. They contacted her and told her that we had asked to see her. To my surprise she agreed to come up to Break for a visit. There was a big buzz of excitement in the home before she arrived. It wasn't often that any of the inmates got reunited with their absent mothers after eight years. When she got there the staff took her through to the sitting room and then they fetched Terry and me to come and meet her.

I don't remember now what I had hoped would happen when I first saw her; perhaps I thought she would burst into tears and throw her arms around me and tell me how much she had missed me and how much she regretted her decision to leave us. I think I wanted to feel an immediate bond with her, something so strong between mother and daughter that even the fact it had been so long since she had seen us wouldn't prevent it from holding firm.

When I walked into the room and saw her for the first time I felt not the slightest spark of recognition or emotion. She could have been anybody they had just dragged in off the street to act the part of my long-lost mother. Having spent so many years listening to Dad telling us about what a beautiful woman she was, I was shocked by her ordinariness. I had allowed myself to be fooled by his rose-tinted spectacles because I had wanted to believe that my mother must be something wonderful. It hadn't just been Dad. Other people who had known them when they were young had told us how stunning she was and what a glamorous couple they had made, so I suppose I had expected to meet the same young woman that they had all talked about, not this woman who was eight years older and worn down by life, stripped of the wigs and dresses and make-up that she had been able to afford when she was on the game rather than working in shops and hotels. Maybe I had imagined that she had left us for a far more glamorous life, away from the day-to-day drudgery of bringing up a family in a council house. After all, if she hadn't run away to a better life, why had she gone? Had it really been so terrible to be with us that it was better to be a hotel chambermaid or a shop girl with no home of her own? So many questions were spinning around inside my head that I didn't know where to start, so I didn't say much.

'Do you want a cup of tea?' I asked to try to break the awkwardness of the encounter.

'Yes, please.'

'Do you take sugar?' I asked, shocked to think that I had to ask my own mother such a fundamental question. It seemed to bring home to me what complete strangers we were. I felt a sudden rush of bitterness towards her for abandoning us and never caring enough to get in touch, never allowing us to get to know her.

She had been driven up to Break by her mum and dad and they had gone off into the local town after dropping her at the home. She asked if we would like to meet them. I thought that was a brilliant idea – maybe they would live up to the idealized pictures I carried in my head. As we walked down the road she pulled out a packet of cigarettes and offered them to us. Even though I'd been smoking since I was eleven, I knew this was an odd thing for a mother to offer her children. It didn't seem like responsible parent-ing. It seemed like she was trying to be pals with us, which wasn't what we wanted. We wanted a proper mother. We still accepted the proffered cigarettes of course because they hardly ever let us smoke at Break, but still it seemed to undermine even further the idea that she was our long-lost mum and that she really cared about us after all. Terry wasn't as cynical as me and was delighted that she was back, but I was holding myself in reserve all through that day.

When we got to the town my grandmother was no more familiar to me than Mum, but for some strange rea-son I recognized my grandfather immediately. Although I didn't realize it at the time, he had apparently always had a bit of a soft spot for me when I was small. I found out later that when Mum left us he had tried to put her mind at rest a little.

'Don't ever worry about that little girl,' he told her, 'she'll be all right.'

I've often wondered what made him think that and why he didn't make any effort to check on me after Mum had gone. Maybe he did and I just didn't hear about it.

After eight years of having no contact with us, Mum suddenly seemed prepared to look after us completely. The plan was that because Dad was in prison it was safe for her to move back up to the area and get a home together for the three of us so we could all live happily ever after. I couldn't believe that it could all be so easy after so many years. Why had we had to wait so long for her to decide to do this? Dad had been to prison before, so surely there had been other opportunities? But I didn't say anything, for fear of putting a doubt into her mind. I really wanted this to happen. Initially, however, she had to go back down to Eastbourne to sort out her affairs and work out her notice before moving north.

Once she had gone and my initial disappointment with her had worn off, I grew more and more excited at the idea of spending more time with her. Whatever had happened in the past she was still our mum, after all, and if we were back with her we would be reunited with our grandparents and other members of the family we hadn't seen since she'd gone. Maybe this way we would actually find a life where we felt we belonged and fitted in. With Dad away we had no other family and the idea of being part of a unit again was wonderful.

I talked about it a lot back at Break with Mel, and the more we talked about it the more impatient I became to see Mum again and get to know her better. A week or so after the visit the two of us cooked up a plan to run away from Break and head for Eastbourne. I imagined Mum would be just as thrilled to see me again as I would be to see her, and I thought she would be flattered to think we had gone to so much trouble to find her.

We got out of the home quite easily and then hitch-hiked down south. Only when we got there did we realize that Eastbourne is quite a large place and we didn't even have any idea where she lived or worked. There was also some sort of carnival going on which meant the streets were full of crowds, making it all seem even more confusing and overwhelming. By systematically trekking around all the hotels along the seafront we eventually managed to find where she was.

'We've come down to visit you,' I said when we were finally taken to see her, feeling so proud of myself for making such a long journey and maybe hoping once again that she would fling her arms round me or at least be touched that I cared enough to make the effort.

'You've run away,' she snapped. 'Now you can bloody well run back.'

It felt like a slap in the face. In the end she grudgingly let us stay the weekend before sending us all the way back to Norwich but she obviously wasn't pleased to be so inconvenienced. When we arrived back I got all the blame from the staff for leading Mel astray, even though our adventure had been a joint decision, but I was used to that. Neither of us would have gone on our own, but I certainly hadn't held a gun to her head. In some ways she was the leader. Terry was the same as me, always getting the blame for everything no matter who else was involved. It was like we were the real 'problem children' while everyone else had some mitigating reason for why they were in care.

One time when Mel was brought back to Break after a holiday she became so depressed she took an overdose. When I saw how much attention she got with that I decided to do the same myself a few weeks later, just as I had when the boy smashed his room up at The Durdans. I managed to save up some paracetamol by telling different staff members I had a headache or period pains, then one night I swallowed them all. I don't remember how many it was but obviously not too many. Of course I didn't get the same attention or sympathy as Mel – I just got told I was being pathetic and to pull myself together.

I've probably taken more than a dozen overdoses through the years, since that first one at the age of fourteen. Every time while I was actually putting the tablets in my mouth I always intended to kill myself, but sometimes I would change my mind a few moments after I'd swallowed them. A kind of survival instinct cuts in. Realizing I didn't really want to die, I would panic and tell someone what I had done, just as Dad used to. They would then raise the alarm and once the attempt had failed I would be left with all the shame and embarrassment of having had my stomach pumped and of being given a load of lectures. With each failed attempt my self-esteem would shrink further.

A few weeks after our reunion Mum moved back up to Norwich so we could live with her and the council gave her a lovely three-bedroom house. It seemed like we were daddy's little earner

actually going to be a normal family after all. Social services furnished and decorated the house, bending over
backwards to give us the best possible start together, and
Terry and I went off to live with her with high hopes. By
that time Mum had explained to us that she was pregnant
by a man she had met down in Eastbourne, but it soon
became obvious that he was not going to be taking
responsibility for his child. Despite our optimism, the
omens for us were not good.

Chapter Fifteen

hardcore

For all Terry's and my good intentions, and maybe Mum's as well, there was little chance that the three of us would be able to establish a relationship after so long apart and after everything that we had all been through along the way. Our new little family unit lasted exactly six weeks and it was a bumpy ride from day one. I don't doubt that both Terry and I were complete pains in the neck for Mum, and that having had no one to worry about but herself for the last eight years it was a bit of a shock to suddenly find herself in charge of two difficult teenagers she hardly knew and who harboured incredible resentments towards her, but it was still a disappointment to find her defeated so easily.

We had changed schools yet again in order to attend one closer to our new home, and I was refusing to go in at all, not wanting to start all over again with people I didn't know. I'd had enough of having to prove myself in new social groups, dealing with new bullies all over again and having to show them who was boss. I just wanted to be left alone and maybe have a bit of fun out of life. I would skive off up to the city with friends instead, drinking and generally playing up. There were a lot of arguments at home as Mum attempted in vain to exercise some sort of parental control, which I counteracted with large doses of adolescent resentment, ending up slashing my wrists and taking an overdose yet again. Social services were called and Mum was forced to admit she couldn't cope with us.

After things had gone wrong with Mum, Terry and I were taken into care again. I was heartbroken that my dreams of having a proper family had come to nothing and I was even more devastated when I was told that Terry and I were going to be separated this time. I was taken to a place called Bramerton Lodge, while Terry was moved into a hostel to have a go at a sort of independent living. I couldn't understand why we weren't both returned to Break and I felt rejected and abandoned by them as well as by my mother. I know my behaviour wasn't great but the things I did – cutting myself, taking overdoses, prostitution, drinking myself into a stupor – were hurting me much more than anyone else. I was crying out for help and no one at all was responding.

Bramerton was a remand and assessment centre in the countryside outside Norwich. It was considered to be the last chance for kids like me, after which prison or borstal were the only options open to us. The building, which had ominous-looking bars at the windows, was stuck in a field in the middle of nowhere. I was told I would be there for just six weeks while they decided what to do with me next, but in fact I would stay there for the best part of three years on and off.

It was completely different to any home I had been in before, with a very strict, controlled routine. My first night there I walked into the common room with a big bolshy attitude.

'How do I get out of this dump?' I asked loudly.

The other kids all laughed, telling me there was no way of getting out; the place was far too secure. On many occasions over the next few years I would prove that it wasn't, but I remember feeling very lonely and scared that night, wondering what on earth was going to happen to me next.

The scenery around Bramerton was beautiful, filled with idyllic, well-cared-for little villages where people lived pleasant tidy lives so unlike mine it was hard to imagine. The place itself, however, was more or less a children's prison. I was forever being locked up and punished for trivial rule breaking like being caught in possession of a cigarette lighter. If we wanted to light our cigarettes we were supposed to ask a member of staff. I suppose they thought we would burn the place down if we had our own lighters, but we could probably have done that with a lighted cigarette almost as easily. On the whole, however, it wasn't a bad place; they even gave us a fag allowance. They had their own little school on the premises, which I hated from the start. Pupils spent their whole time making moccasins or nailing felt to boards, a bit like prisoners sewing mail bags, none of which I had any time for and the teacher seemed really up himself.

Initially I spent six weeks there while they tried to work out what to do with me next. They soon discovered, however, that no one else wanted to take me on and that they were pretty much stuck with me. It's not hard to see why. On paper I did not look like a very good bet. It was common knowledge by then that I was on the game and it was on the record that I kept running away from anywhere they took me to, trying to get back to my dad who was the source of all my problems. I guess I ran away all the time partly because Dad told me to, but also partly because that was what Mum had done with us and because I never felt like I belonged anywhere so there was no reason to resist the temptation to move on. I was always hoping that the grass would be greener somewhere else, despite constant disappointments. And wherever they put me I always wanted to escape back to Dad, the one place where I felt I belonged, however horrible the reality of it might end up being once I got there.

Social services had tried many times to get me back into mainstream schooling but I would always decide I hated my new school and would spend my days skiving off and drinking tea with a group of people who used to hang around the city centre. That was how I ended up being put in Bramerton – but despite the warnings from the other kids, I found it wasn't too hard to escape from there when I wanted to head back into the city centre.

It wasn't long after I arrived at Bramerton before I struck up a relationship with a man nearly twenty years older than me. It's surprising how many men are willing to get involved with a young girl in care. He even asked me to marry him and bought an engagement ring from his friend's catalogue. Apart from the fact I was still only fourteen, he should maybe have picked up the signals that whenever he tried to have sex with me I would cry and panic. Social services were writing reports saying how promiscuous I was, but actually I hated sex and it seems quite obvious now that I wanted older men like this guy to be father figures to me. I was looking for love and pro-tection in all the wrong places and in completely the wrong ways.

In December that year Mum gave birth to my baby brother, Adam, and I went to the hospital with my new boyfriend to visit them. Things between Mum and me were very strained; I don't think we'd even spoken since Terry and I had been taken back into care, so the visit was a little awkward, but my new brother was the most adorable thing I had ever seen; he was so beautiful and I loved him at once. That's when I got the idea in my head that it would be wonderful to have a baby of my own to care for.

It soon became obvious, though, that I wasn't really welcome to visit and that I wasn't going to be a part of Mum's or Adam's lives. Since leaving us back when I was six, she had never sent Christmas or birthday cards and that had always hurt. After our failed reunion and subsequent separation again I hoped with all my heart that the door could be left open with Mum, but when no card arrived that Christmas I knew for sure she didn't want me. Mum had said that she was determined to be a brilliant mum to Adam as she had screwed it up with her other kids and she wasn't going to do the same with this one. I can honestly say I was never jealous of my baby brother – I have never resented him, but I did her. From the moment we left her new house Mum cut us off as completely as she had when she first left us. We got no calls, no cards, no letters and no visits. It was like we had ceased to exist for her once more. I tried writing letters to her but I received no response. I suppose she was hoping to make a clean start with her new baby and didn't want any of the ugliness of the past to intrude.

It was at this point that I gave up on everything. I felt I had finally lost everyone, even Terry Junior. Social services had told me that there wasn't a children's home or foster home in the county that would take me. It felt as though everyone had given up on me, although I guess they were doing the best they could to find a solution to an almost impossible problem.

Escaping had become like second nature to me. As soon as I saw an opportunity to get back to Dad, if he was out of jail, or back to my friends in the city pubs, I would take it. I dare say it was also obvious to anyone with experience in dealing with difficult teenagers that I had started doing drugs as well as drinking. In Bramerton I was mixing with some pretty hardcore people aged from twelve up to eighteen. We used to sniff glue and aerosols, none of us wanting to say 'no' when it was offered and risk looking like wimps. I never liked it, particularly the glue, because it only gave you a hit for a few seconds and then left you with a nasty headache. Aerosols weren't so bad, but I preferred more grown-up drugs if I could get hold of them. Through my friends in the pubs I got hold of cannabis and tried that, then I moved on to speed, which would become my drug of choice for the next few years.

I was generally pretty uncooperative and difficult with anyone who tried to tell me what to do. I guess the refusing to do what people told me stemmed from having Dad ordering me around for so many years, bullying me into doing things that I really didn't want to do. If people asked me nicely I could be cooperative, but the sort of people who worked in a place like Bramerton didn't always have the time or inclination for such niceties, which meant I didn't always react well to them. The couple who ran the home, Mr and Mrs Mcquarrie, kept their distance from me at first but I remember I was always nervous if I was called up to see them for some misdemeanour or other. Mr Mcquarrie was the sort of man who automatically commanded respect, a man with a headmasterly presence.

Most of the anger that I had boiling away inside me was directed towards myself. I was often slashing my wrists or other parts of my body in self-disgust, taking overdoses or sitting in a bath tub trying to scrape myself clean with neat bleach and a scrubbing brush, not bothered that I was rubbing so hard I was drawing blood. Some of the other girls were anorexic and bulimic and I was just as convinced as they were that I was overweight and I used to long to be like them. I would try to make myself sick after meals, as I saw them doing, but it never worked. I would push my fingers down my throat but it would only make me gag, I could never actually rid myself of any food. My body repelled me because Dad had repeatedly told me how fat and ugly it was, and because of the way it had been bought and sold so cheaply, used and disposed of over and over again by anyone with ten pounds and a few minutes to spare.

There was a fashion amongst the girls at Bramerton for tattooing one another with needles and Indian ink.

The staff didn't take much notice of that sort of thing; I suppose it was a pretty harmless pastime compared with suicide attempts and arson. I actually tattooed the word 'Dad' on my forearm because I still felt I belonged to him and truly believed I always would. I started out doing it with a needle and ink but it was taking so long I got bored and finished the job off by slashing clumsily away with a Stanley blade.

Having learnt my lesson that day back at junior school when I turned on the bullies who were picking on me, I was determined to establish a reputation for being the hardest girl in Bramerton so that I would never get into a position where I might be bullied. I'd had enough of being a victim at Dad's hands and with scumbags like his mate Pete and all the pathetic punters in their shiny motors. I wasn't willing to accept it from anyone else, ever. I hated violence but I knew that I would have to establish my credentials amongst these hard cases if I wanted to avoid being picked on and beaten up the whole time. Over time I became top dog amongst the girls, partly because I was there longer than most other people and knew my way around, and partly because I protected my position with my fists.

I made sure my reputation amongst the girls was established quickly, showing that I would never be afraid to use violence under any circumstances if I was pushed. I must have been convincing because I hardly ever had to actually fight; just fronting up to people was enough, but I knew I had to be prepared to prove how hard I really was at any time. Every new girl who came in was going to test the boundaries to see if she would be able to take over my spot at the top of the pile. I could never allow that to happen.

I wasn't a bully at all myself. I would never pick on anyone weaker than me. I was more of an agony aunt to most of them, but now and again I had to assert my authority and stick up for myself because someone was challenging my authority. I felt the other girls were constantly watching to see how I reacted to challenges, waiting for me to show a weakness.

After I had been there a few months a new girl grassed me up for something – I can't remember what – and a crowd formed with the other girls who knew me threatening her that I would beat her up after lights out. It was almost as though they were proud of how hard I was and looked forward to watching how I was going to show this upstart the error of her ways, putting her in her place. Grassing on anyone was a cardinal sin in a place like Bramerton so I knew they were going to expect me to dole out some sort of punishment. I hoped that if I came on aggressively enough the new girl would crack and apologize and quickly prove that she had no bottle. I would then be able to just issue a warning and walk away without doing any damage. I had a feeling from the disdainful looks she was giving me and the mocking tone of her voice, however, that she wasn't going to be that sort of girl. She was going to be prepared to call my bluff.

I was feeling sick with anticipation of what I was going to have to do as a group of us went to her bedroom that night, psyched up like an adolescent lynch mob. I didn't want to have to do anything but I could tell from her attitude as she faced us down that she was after my position and she wasn't going to back away. She was out to prove how tough she was, just as I was, and it was reaching a point where it would look like weakness in either of us if we conceded any ground. I knew I was going to have to use violence and in the heat of the argument I acted instinctively, picking up a piece of broken glass and threatening to slash her face. Even as the words came out of my mouth I was praying she would back down because I really didn't want to do it. The thought of slashing anyone's face made me feel terrified. I would rather have just punched her but I had made my stand and reached a point where I couldn't actually drop the piece of glass without looking soft.

The other girls were baying for blood, goading me on, accusing me of 'losing it'. I really, really didn't want to do it but I couldn't think how to get out of the situation without losing the high ground. My mind was racing and I was buzzing with adrenaline. There wasn't time to try to reason my way out of the situation. Making a snap decision I slashed the edge of the broken glass across her hand rather than her face. I wish I'd had the courage to tell them all to fuck off, put the glass down and walked away, but I wasn't ready for that. The blood flowed from her cut and all hell broke loose as the girl became hysterical and the staff were called. They came running and my victim was rushed away to hospital for stitches. They marched me off to a little room downstairs and locked me in.

One member of staff, a man who really hated me, was so pleased that I had finally overstepped the mark he couldn't stop himself from gloating: 'We've got you now, Maria. You're going to Holloway now.' (The notorious women's prison was always a threat they hung over me.)

I thought he was probably right but I felt so bad about what I had done and the sort of person I had become that I really didn't care any more. I thought I deserved to go to prison.

The staff called the police who took me away for a night in the cells. In court the next morning, Mr and Mrs Mcquarrie turned up to give evidence. Seeing them made me even more certain that I was on my way to prison. I knew that they all thought I was out of hand and this would be their big chance to get shot of me. To my surprise, Mr Mcquarrie stood up in court and fought tooth and nail to get me remanded back to Bramerton, arguing that if I went to Holloway I would be on a downhill road that I would probably never recover from.

I felt so guilty about what I had done that even I thought I deserved to go to prison but Mr Mcquarrie's pleadings swayed the court and they agreed that I should be taken back to Bramerton and given another chance. The other girl was moved somewhere else for her own safety, which didn't seem fair to me, but the whole incident cemented my reputation as someone you didn't mess with unless you wanted to end up hurt, humiliated and shipped out.

I realized that the Mcquarries had put their necks on the line for me and it was a real wake-up call. I believed they were right in what they said and that if I had gone to Holloway it would have been the end of the line for me. I would have become like the other women in there and would have been destined for a life of violence and crime from the moment I walked through the door. As well as being surprised, I was deeply grateful and moved that they had stuck up for me. Not many people had ever spoken out for me before.

Soon after that, Mrs Mcquarrie came to see me one day when I was working in the kitchens and she invited me to sit down and have a fag with her in her office. This soon became a regular thing; she invited me into her office most days to have cups of coffee and cigarettes with her like we were friends. Other members of staff used to come in and tell me it was time to go into school but she would stick up for me.

'No,' she would brush them aside, 'she's all right. I've got a little job for her later.'

I used to love watching her in action. She only had one hand because of an accident when she was young. Although she had a false hand she never used it but it was amazing what she could do one-handed, the phone wedged between her shoulder and her ear, a cigarette dangling from the corner of her mouth and writing something at the same time. It would make me laugh just to watch her juggling all her jobs at once.

She and her husband showed me a lot of kindness after saving me from prison. I think I must have become a bit of a pet project for them. The Christmas after Mum had kicked us out, I had nowhere to go during the holiday period. I confided in Mrs Mcquarrie about how hurt I was that Mum never got in touch with us.

'Why don't you send her a card?' she suggested. 'You're a grown-up too now; maybe you could make the first move towards another reconciliation.'

I did as she suggested, but I still didn't hear anything back. Mum couldn't have made it any clearer that she wanted nothing more to do with us. All the other children at Bramerton were going back to friends and relatives for the holiday and there was just going to be me and a lovely lad called Martin left behind. To my total astonishment, the Mcquarries did this amazing thing: they sent their entire staff home and stayed at Bramerton themselves instead of going to their own house in Norwich. On Christmas Day they brought Martin and me breakfast in bed and turned the dining room into a proper family room, bringing in their family Christmas tree and decorations and buying us both presents. I've still got the silver bangle they gave me. After lunch we sat around watching television together. They could have employed staff to deal with us but they chose instead to give up their own Christmas break for us. It still hurt to think that our families didn't want us but it was so touching that the Mcquarries would do that for us, especially when I had given them nothing but trouble. I was overwhelmed by the gesture, feeling that I was unworthy of it, but they couldn't have been nicer.

On the Boxing Day of that year another little girl had to come back to join us because her baby nephew had died of a cot death, which made me feel less sorry for myself. So many people in Bramerton were in an even worse state than me. For years afterwards I would hear about other children I knew during those years and there would be stories of how they were now heavily into their drugs or in prison or dead. Many of them had been too damaged at the start of their lives to be able to cope with the pressures of the real world once they were forced to go out into it.

I may have started to get closer to Mrs Mcquarrie but it didn't make me calm down and become an angel overnight. There was an incident with another girl in Bramerton, which added even more to my reputation as someone you shouldn't mess with. This girl was on the game too, so she must have been pretty tough. We always had to wait outside the dining room before we were allowed to go in for meals and when I asked her before one meal what the time was she was really rude to me.

'Whatever is your fucking problem?' I wanted to know. 'Don't talk to me like that.'

'You think you're so special…' she spat back.

She was still mouthing off as we went in and took our places round one of the big circular tables. She sat down opposite me, carefully poured herself a cup of tea, stood up and threw it over me. I sat for a few seconds, dripping and gathering my thoughts. I then stood up, picked up the giant teapot which was filled and ready to serve the whole table, lifted the lid and hurled the entire contents at her, flooding the beautiful laminate floor which had to be buffed every day to keep its shine, and leaving no one in any doubt that I wasn't going to be pushed around without fighting back. Fortunately the tea wasn't hot enough to cause scalding, but it was uncomfortable all the same. Everyone else at the table leapt up as the tidal wave of hot liquid exploded across them and the staff were trying to get to me in order to restrain me before I attacked the girl again, all of them slipping and sliding around on the wet floor while the boys cheered and jeered their encouragement.

'Go on, Ria!'

It was like a slapstick scene from a Laurel and Hardy movie. We both got punished for that outburst but I didn't feel as guilty as I did about the glassing, partly because she had been the first one to throw the tea but mainly because it had been so funny watching everyone falling about, and because no one ended up being badly hurt.

Not surprisingly I didn't trust any men at that age and I could be pretty horrible to any that crossed my path and displeased me. Dad had always told me how you couldn't trust the men who worked in children's homes because they were all perverts and I believed him. Looking back now I know there were some really nice chaps working in the homes who I didn't give a chance to; men who genuinely wanted to help troubled youngsters like me. There had been one male carer at Break who I was always accusing of trying to see me in the bath although looking back I'm sure nothing of the sort had ever crossed his mind.

Having said that, there were a few men who made the girls feel uneasy at Bramerton. We weren't allowed to have any locks on our doors so we had no privacy and there were certain members of staff who seemed to pop up from nowhere, hovering around the corridors during bath times. There was one man who we knew used to take his shoes off to sneak upstairs at the time when we were all getting undressed for bed, so we sprinkled drawing pins on the steps and listened gleefully to his muffled exclamations and shouts of pain as he stepped on them in his stockinged feet.

There was one carer who particularly hated me. The home was built in a square with a house at each corner, all joined by corridors. At one corner was the laundry and the offices, on another the boys' dormitory, then the girls' section and finally a mixed-sex family type of set-up. There were five or six bedrooms in the girls' part, a sitting room and a kitchen. At the end of each house was a staff flat and this chap, who was a big ex-soldier, lived in the girls' house with his wife and children, who we never saw. I was intimidated by him but determined not to let him know it, so I tried to aggravate him as much as I could.

We were meant to put our lights out and settle down at ten o'clock but we would deliberately make a lot of noise after that, just to wind him up. One night at about midnight he completely lost the plot and came storming in, ordering everyone out of their beds, even the girls who were innocently sleeping. He lined us up along the corridor and was screaming and spitting into my face, his complexion bright scarlet, while I was just standing laughing at him. I knew he wanted to hit me but he couldn't without losing his job and ending up in court and I exploited his impotence mercilessly. Because I had been brought up to obey Dad or suffer the physical consequences, people who were put in positions of authority over me but weren't allowed to touch me had real trouble making me do anything I didn't want to do. It must have driven that one guy absolutely crazy, but he had to back down or risk losing his job.

If I liked a carer I might try to please them, but I just wanted to give the others a hard time. Maybe I was taking revenge for all the times Dad had beaten me when I had done nothing wrong, trying to even up the scales in a warped kind of a way.

Bramerton was only meant to be for short stays, but I was there almost solidly between the ages of fourteen and seventeen. A couple of times they tried to move me on to halfway-house establishments where I could live independently within a community, to try to prepare me for coping on my own in the outside world, but the first time that happened I was accused of stealing some money, which I never did, and the second time I was accused of drug dealing because I scored some acid for two other girls while I was in town. So both times I ended up back at Bramerton again, feeling like a failure.

It was surprising that anyone still held out any hope for me at all by that stage. It looked as though I was doomed to be in a downward spiral forever, just like in the nightmare I used to have when I lived with Dad, falling into nothingness, certain that it could only end with my death.

Chapter Sixteen

meeting brian

I was still escaping from Bramerton whenever the opportunity presented itself and sometimes I went to stay with Dad if he was out of jail at the time, because he put a lot of pressure on me to get back to him whenever I could. However, I was beginning to resent working on the block and handing the money over to him when I could just keep it for myself if he wasn't around. Anyway, I preferred meeting up with my friends in town. There was a cafeteria where unemployed people used to sit smoking and making a cup of tea last all morning and I met a few people there. When I was on the run from Break or Bramerton, and if I wasn't with Dad or Kathy, I never really cared who I stayed with as long as they were friendly and there was plenty to drink or swallow. Most of the people I ended up staying with I would meet and bond with in pubs, while both of us were mellowed by alcohol.

I was fifteen when I met a guy called John who let me stay for a few weeks at his place in the suburbs of the city. People who drink together are often generous in that way, like Dad used to be with friends such as Lucy. I never had sex with him. Since I was having sex with men for money and not enjoying it, I wasn't in a hurry to do it for nothing as well unless I fancied myself to be in love – not even for friends who were being generous with accommodation. I remember this guy had a bread van and I used to go with him on his delivery rounds sometimes. I had been there several weeks before he tried it on with me one night. I wasn't having any of that. I'd had enough of men wanting to have sex with me – what I wanted was friends I could have a laugh with who didn't want anything from me, so I stormed out of his house at about six in the morning, probably shouting something about 'that' being all men ever wanted from me and slamming the door after me. With self-esteem as near rock bottom as mine was in those days it wasn't hard for people to offend me. I was always on the look out for more evidence of how low my position in the world was and how little I should expect by way of respect from anyone.

Having made my sad little moral stand I was then without a place to stay and was walking down this road I didn't recognize as dawn broke. Unsure where I was going to go next, I heard someone wolf whistling. Since there was no one else around I could be pretty sure it was directed at me. I looked around for the culprit to give him a piece of my mind. The only person in view was a friendly looking bearded man with long dark hair leaning over the balcony of his first-floor flat, grinning down at me. I must have recognized something good in him straight away because I didn't give him an earful as I might have done in the circumstances, and we got talking.

'Why don't you come up?' he suggested after a minute or two. Since I had no other plans and he seemed a congenial sort, I did.

His name, I discovered, was Brian and he was an Irish biker who'd been banned from driving and had had to get rid of his bike, leaving him stranded in suburbia just like me. He might have been without any wheels but there was no doubting that he was still a biker in style and spirit. It turned out he was thirty-five years old, a full twenty years older than me. He was tall and slim and nice-looking, at least I thought so. His flat seemed to be full of people, some of them lodgers, some of them just friends passing through, who gradually stirred into life during the next few hours, all of them looking rumpled and hung over as they appeared from under blankets and inside sleeping bags.

Brian was a bit of an artist and he had painted a huge Motorhead skull on the wall above the fireplace. It was an exact copy of the original fanged face created for the heavy metal rockers by an artist called Joe Petango. Brian had surrounded it with his own twisting patterns of drag-ons and flames. There were more examples of his art-work on his body, and one of his arms was completely covered in tattoos that he'd designed himself. He had a rose on his neck, which wasn't like any tattoo I'd ever seen before, especially not the amateurish slashings I'd inflicted on my own body. Everything about Brian seemed to be unique and interesting and part of his personality.

He also had a miniature Yorkshire terrier called Motorhead-Dick-the-Shit, or 'Dick' for short. Dick was the tiniest dog with the biggest personality imaginable. He was impossible to train and impossible to get cross with, even when he chewed up my cigarettes on that first morning of our acquaintance. I'm not sure who I fell in love with first, Brian or Dick, but together they were irresistible.

Even more irresistible, however, was one of the other boys loafing about the flat. Since I had nowhere else to go I just stayed until I was caught out on the street a few days later and sent back to Bramerton once more, by which time this lad was officially my new boyfriend – at least in my mind. While we were together we spent all our time drinking and taking drugs, which suited me fine, and the moment we were parted I pined like any lovesick teenag-er. I believed I had found someone who loved me and I was high on having proved Dad wrong again.

Eager to get back to my new love I escaped from Bramerton again as soon as I possibly could, but when I arrived
at the flat I discovered my wonderful new 'boyfriend' had
grown tired of waiting and was already going with another girl, which left me devastated as usual, convinced yet
again that Dad had been right after all and that no man
would ever want me for anything except easy sex. In my
despair I turned to Brian for comfort and his gentle wisdom and kindness overwhelmed me. I realized I had just
picked the wrong man. Brian, I decided, was the one for
me. He wasn't much younger than Dad; maybe it was a
father figure I had been craving all along when I had tried
to get all those poor frustrated schoolboys to declare their
undying devotion.

As I got to know him better I found out more about
Brian's history. He told me how his dad had beaten him
about when he was a kid and had ended up running off
with a prostitute, a blow Brian said that his devoutly
Catholic mother had never really recovered from. His
brother and sister had gone on to lead quite straight lives,
not like Brian. He had tried to be like them, he even built
up his own decorating business, got married and bought a
house, but one day he'd realized he didn't want any of it,
that he craved instead to be a free spirit in the world, an
'easy rider'. He became a bit of a rebel and gave everything up to have an affair with another girl, which had
lasted for seven years. The girl kept having miscarriages,

which had put a terrible strain on the relationship until eventually they broke up and Brian started drinking heavily. He still did drink, but he wasn't a nasty drunk like Dad, more like a benevolent one. Nothing seemed to bother Brian much. He was just a lovely, gentle person, easy to be with, philosophical about life's ups and downs and happy in his own skin. When you were with him nothing was ever a problem or a rush.

By that time I had also discovered that two of the girls who had been in the flat on the first day I arrived were on the game too, so it didn't come as a shock to Brian to find out all about what I did for a living. I found I could talk to him about anything, telling him all about Dad and why I kept running away from Bramerton. He had problems of his own, being an alcoholic, but he never let them get him down and they seemed to make him more open and tolerant of other people's mistakes and shortcomings. He had none of Dad's bitterness or anger or need to manipulate and control those around him. We took a lot of magic mushrooms and speed together. Speed in particular made me feel very happy and confident, but it was expensive and meant that I had to stay on the game in order to have the cash to buy it. I was soon taking up to a gram a day, which is a pretty heavy habit for anyone, let alone a fifteen year old.

Speed would keep me high for hours but the comedown was always horrendous, making me immediately want more. For every hour that I felt great there were three or four hours when I felt like shit. I guess it was just luck that I didn't end up becoming dependent on it like so many of the other girls on the street. It also curbs your appetite, which I thought would help me lose weight, but at the same time it rots your gums and produces all sorts of other horrible side effects. I'd seen all these symptoms on other people but I didn't care. I hated myself and my body anyway, so why should I care if I was risking destroying it? I used to take the speed in my drinks, or wrap it in paper and swallow it. My dealer told me I would save money by moving on to cocaine because then I would get the same high with less powder, but I knew that would be one step further on the slippery downward slope and stuck with the drugs I knew. I guess I must have had some sense of self-preservation deep down. In fact, I found out later that he was lying because cocaine would have ended up costing me much more. Thankfully I never got into heroin, which was less freely available and more expensive in those days than it is now.

I was always aware that the feelings the drugs gave me were false, that if I couldn't be happy just because the sun was shining and because I was who I was then there was something more fundamentally wrong with me than any drugs could ever hope to put right, but I had no idea what I should do about it or who I should turn to for help apart from Brian. It was all about escaping from who I was and how I felt, at least for those short periods when I was high. At one stage I even tried sniffing amyl nitrate, which is a deeply scary drug that makes your heart race seconds after you take it, but I didn't rate the effect of that very highly.

I didn't want to be a prostitute then any more than I had done the first night that Dad held me down for Pete to have his way, but I had grown used to the whole routine of it by then, particularly the easy money, and I couldn't work out how to survive financially without it. What sort of job could I have done that would have given me anything like enough money to buy the drink and drugs I needed to keep me from thinking about the reality of my life and from wanting to kill myself? I wonder if there is anything in life that you can't grow accustomed to eventually. I knew it was dangerous to be climbing into cars with strange men and that I was risking my life every time I did it but I didn't care. When you have no love or respect for yourself the thought that you might die doesn't worry you. Just as every time I dropped a tab of acid I knew that it might be the one to kill me, I would just shrug the dangers off, thinking that an accidental death might save me having to go to the effort of killing myself in any more gruesome way.

I got on really well with the other two girls in Brian's house and some days we would go up to the block to work together. One afternoon one of them was walking with me when a guy approached us, telling us how beautiful we were and how we should do some modelling. Given how fat and ugly I always believed I was, his words easily worked their magic. It sounded like a laugh so we went to the address he gave us and had some pictures taken, behaving like two silly, vain teenage girls. He asked if we would be willing to do some shots just in our underwear and because he was being very sweet and flattering we agreed.

'Wow, you could make a fortune,' he enthused as he kept snapping away, encouraging us to touch one another in a fairly innocent sort of way.

'That's as far as we go,' we told him once we'd had enough.

'I've just got to show these to my man,' he said as we were leaving, 'and maybe I can sell them. Come back tomorrow and perhaps we can do some more pictures and draw up a contract.'

Flattered and excited and eager to believe that we had found an easy path to fame and fortune, we went back the next day and he said he needed to take a few more pictures.

'What about all this money you were talking about?' we wanted to know. 'And the contract?'

'We need to see a few more photos,' he said. 'Just slip your bras off.'

That was when we came to our senses and realized we were 'giving it away for free' just like Dad was always saying. Deciding it had gone far enough we ignored his protestations and left; he suddenly seemed like any other punter who didn't want to pay for his kicks.

I often wonder what happened to those pictures and whether they'll turn up on the internet one day. Despite our youth we were both experienced prostitutes, used to dealing with scumbags like Dad, so I would imagine that millions of more innocent young girls must fall for that sort of scam every day and end up being talked into doing things they don't really want to do and later regret. The world is full of predators eager to exploit the inexperience of people who are still children really, even if they look like adults.

I loved being with Brian, absolutely loved it. He was my first real boyfriend and he introduced me to a whole new world. There was the music of people like Bruce Spring-steen, Meatloaf and Bob Seger to start with. He used to play Springsteen's 'Hungry Heart' over and over again on the pub jukebox, just as Dad used to play Charlie Rich. It seemed the most beautiful song in the world to me, and lines like 'Took a wrong turn and just kept going' and 'Ain't nobody wants to be alone' seemed so apt for the lives we were living. Good rock music, like drink and drugs, allows dreamers like Brian to escape just a little from the mundane realities of their lives and imagine they are the free spirits they always wanted to be.

Brian never had to work at being the centre of attention when he was in a pub, as Dad did; people just automatically gravitated towards him because he was a good, kind, laid-back man who treated everyone the same. I convinced myself I was deeply in love and even though I was still only fifteen I managed to persuade a tattoo parlour to engrave 'Property of Brian' on my upper arm, above Dad's name. I was eager to truly belong to someone, especially someone like Brian who would love me and be kind to me and protect me, rather than someone like Dad who just wanted to use and exploit me.

Sometimes I would bump into Dad on the street when I was waiting for punters on the block and it always freaked me out. He was utterly furious that I was working independently of him and that I had switched my loyalties from him to Brian, and I was scared of what he might do to me. When I was feeling brave I told myself there wasn't much he could do unless he was willing to beat me up on the street in front of everyone, or drag me back home with him, which wouldn't have been too good for his image as the caring single father struggling to do the best for his broken family.

As he saw it he'd invested time in me, waiting for me to be old enough to provide a return and now I wasn't paying my dues to him. He'd planned for me to provide him with a free meal ticket for years, just as he had with Mum, and I guess he thought I had let him down exactly like she had.

Knowing I had Brian to go back to made me brave enough to stand up to Dad a bit. As long as he couldn't get me home on my own I felt I was reasonably safe, but you never knew with him. I was always aware there was a danger that he might come lurching out of the pub one night all liquored up and looking for a fight. Brian knew all about him and what he had done to me and I knew he would stand up for me if I asked him to, but I was constantly aware that Dad could pounce at any time when I was on my own. I had known him beat up enough people in my life, including me, to be sure that he was capable of anything when his pride, reputation and financial interests were threatened.

Funnily enough, although there's no question that he hated Brian, Dad never tried to attack him physically. Probably he wasn't confident that he would have come off best.

Although he was twenty years older than me I don't doubt for a minute that Brian loved me. He always wanted to protect and look after me and we had a wonderful time together. There was a pub we used to go to all the time where the landlady knew all about us. She was aware how young I was but was still willing to serve me as much vodka as I could drink. On the day that Brian and I bought a silver ring down the market and announced we were getting engaged, she and everyone else in the bar were delighted. I was ecstatic, of course. I thought I was getting the one thing I'd always wanted: a proper family, someone who loved me, who I could rely on.

I'd spend some time with Brian and then I'd get caught and taken back to Bramerton, but I'd always try to escape again as soon as I could and return to him. I was still only fifteen so social services decided that Bramerton wasn't able to hold me and I should be sent to a secure unit in Peterborough called Salter's Lodge. They couldn't put me in prison because I hadn't actually committed any crimes but they had to do something to show they were protecting me from myself and from those around me who they saw as dangerous predators. I was terrified, having been told all sorts of stories about secure units by other kids and how they would put me in a straitjacket if I caused any trouble.

When I arrived at Salter's Lodge on a Friday the staff told me they didn't have a bed ready in the secure unit until the Monday so they were going to have to put me in another section, which was a sort of halfway house a bit like Bramerton, until they were ready to transfer me. What that meant was that I had a weekend in which to get away or I would be effectively trapped behind bars for as long as they wanted to keep me there. I could see the main building from where I was housed and to my eyes it looked exactly like an adult prison. I enjoyed my life with Brian too much to be willing to be locked away in there without a fight but I said nothing, just watching and waiting for my chance.

That weekend the staff were taking all the children from the halfway house out to Skegness to go roller skating.

'One of us is going to have to stay here with you all evening,' they told me grumpily, 'because you can't be trusted, which has really pissed us off because we'd all like to go.'

'That's not my fault,' I retorted. 'It's your job. It's what you get paid for. It's up to you whether you trust me or not.'

'If we could trust you,' they wheedled, 'you could come with us.'

'Well,' I said, as reasonably as I could manage, 'how are you ever going to learn to trust me if you don't give me a chance?'

For some bizarre reason they believed me, despite my record for running away at every opportunity, and agreed to take me with them. They must really have wanted that night out. The moment we arrived in Skegness they all got into the holiday spirit and seemed to forget that I was famous for absconding and needed to be watched every second of the day. I simply wandered off the moment their backs were turned, hitchhiked back to Norwich and went straight to Brian's flat.

The police came looking for me early the following

morning, banging on the front door while Brian lowered me out of a first-floor window at the back. I legged it down the road and met up with him again once the police had searched the flat and gone away empty-handed. Whenever I was with Brian life seemed like one big hilarious adventure, but there was a serious edge to our escape plans this time because I really didn't want to be caught and incarcerated in Salter's Lodge.

Brian wanted to be with me as much as I wanted to be with him. He believed that social services were letting me down and that I needed to be got away from Norwich and away from the danger of Dad getting his hands on me, so we decided to run away together. The plan was that we would hitch down to London and Brian would find work as a painter and decorator to support us until I was old enough for us to return to Norwich and live legally as a couple.

I was so flattered that he would be willing to do such a thing for me that I didn't stop to think about the practicalities of the trip. He had a very comfortable life in Norwich and yet he was willing to give it up and run off with a fifteen-year-old girl, risking getting into trouble himself in the process. No one had ever offered to do anything like that for me in the past. Why would I hesitate for even a second before putting my fate into his hands?

Chapter Seventeen

the streets of king's cross

Swinging his rucksack onto his back and tucking Dick-the-Shit into the front of his leather jacket as usual, Brian led me to a roundabout leading to the London road and we settled down on the verge to wait for a lift. Almost the first vehicle to appear was a police motorbike and for a moment I thought the game was up before we'd even managed to get out of the town. But as we watched in amazement the bike tilted, went into an uncontrollable skid and toppled over, dragging the poor rider along the tarmac with it. All Brian's good biker instincts came to the fore immediately at the sight of a fellow traveller in trouble. Thrusting Dick into my arms he told me to go into the nearby park while he helped the policeman. It was a typical Brian gesture, the sort of thing that made him popular with everyone he met.

Once the policeman had been safely removed in an ambulance and the fuss had died down, we took our positions again and headed south in the first truck that stopped for us. We were in no particular hurry to get to London and Brian was always open to new experiences when he was on his travels. He had a little one-man tent in his rucksack so we could stop off wherever we wanted to and pitch our own private camp, squeezing into the tent together to sleep. As we still had a bit of money in our pockets from his last giro and my earnings from the street, we spent a couple of days in Banham, a village that boasts a famous cider house, and got absolutely sloshed, living in our tent in the woods like a couple of runaway kids. It all seemed to be a great adventure and I always felt so safe with Brian, confident that he would protect me from any danger.

When we finally arrived in London we took the tube to King's Cross, which Brian knew was a place where we might be able to find cheap accommodation. I'm sure he genuinely was trying to save me from Dad and from incarceration in Salter's Lodge, but it probably wasn't the best idea for us to head straight to one of the most infamous red light districts in the country.

It didn't really matter how cheap the accommodation was because by then we'd spent all the money we had set out with. With nowhere to stay and no money in our pockets we just wandered around the streets talking to people who looked as though they might inhabit the same sort of world as us, until eventually someone told us about a squat they had heard of in a derelict house which might be worth investigating. Our luck was in and when we got there we were told there was one small room still going spare on the ground floor. Even by our standards the house was in a pretty disgusting state, but at least it was a roof over our heads and it took us off the streets. A tent is of limited use when you're in the middle of a city. We didn't fancy sleeping rough and we could hardly turn up at a homeless shelter given that I was underage and on the run.

There was a sink in the room with a cold tap that dribbled all the time. There was nowhere else in the house for us to wash or shower and I only had the one set of clothes that I had run away from Salter's Lodge in. Each night I had to wash out my one pair of knickers, scrubbing at them with a bar of soap as I'd seen Nanny do so many times at her kitchen sink. It was a bit like being a child again, surviving between Nanny's weekly washing sessions, only worse because there were no clean clothes waiting for us at the end of each week. My spirits were pretty low but I still hoped Brian would be able to find work and look after me, as we had agreed.

To give him his due, he did his best to look for work so we could buy some food, but he just couldn't find anything. I guess by then neither of us looked or smelled particularly appealing. It soon became obvious that the only option left open to us was for me to go on the game to get a bit of money together so that at least we wouldn't starve. It was a scary prospect but hunger was scarier. The grubby, manic streets of King's Cross were a thousand times more terrifying than the block in Norwich, and I no longer had Dad's reputation to protect me when I was out there, parading around for business. I was just one more runaway teenager amongst hundreds, a truly disposable item in the desperate marketplace for youthful flesh. If one of my punters had decided to kill me and dispose of my body who would have known or cared? Only Brian and Dick-the-Shit, and who would have taken any notice of anything Brian had to say when he was the guy who had brought me there in the first place?

Most of the time I got myself high on speed or acid before I went out to work just so that I could overcome my fears, but the drugs cost even more money and meant I had to service more punters. It was like I was sleepwalking through a bad dream, doing everything by rote just as Dad had taught me to, not wanting to allow myself to think too much about what I was doing and where it was likely to lead me. The other prostitutes working in King's Cross all looked older and harder and more vicious than any of the girls I had ever met in Norwich. There was no one here like Lucy. These were people who everyone had given up on, junkies and schizophrenics and God alone

knew what else. I'd never really known many black people before, apart from Gail, and I didn't understand the
way they or their pimps acted or talked to me. I couldn't
tell the difference between their normal speech patterns
and threatening behaviour. It was like occupying an alien
landscape, where I was unable to read or understand any
of the signs around me; everything seemed strange and
dangerous, angry and aggressive.

The routine of walking up to kerb-crawling cars was
exactly the same as it had been in Ber Street, but there
was no local country lane to take the punters to now, just
scruffy back streets and seedy hotel rooms that could be
rented by the hour. The street where I worked looked a
bit like Albert Square from *EastEnders*, with seats in the
centre surrounded by black railings and a path all round
the outside, full of furtive shadows, litter and parked
cars. I was so intimidated by the manic activity and the
aggression all around me that I would only do one trick
at a time, earning just enough so we could buy some food
and some drugs, scurrying back to Brian and Dick as
soon as it was over and then not going back out there
again until the money had run out and we were hungry
once more. It wasn't like working for Dad, where I
would have to stay out until the last client had gone
home; I was my own boss now, I could do as many or as
few as I wanted. Except I wasn't really the boss – hunger
was the one in charge.

One of the pimps on the street, a black guy dripping in charm and gold jewellery, was being quite flirty and nice with me one afternoon when I was looking for business. There wasn't much going on. The punters were always more discreet in the daylight and because I was new to the area I wasn't able to recognize the regulars unless they made themselves obvious, which put me at a disadvantage.

'Do you need any help?' he asked cheerily.

'Well,' I admitted reluctantly, 'yeah.'

'I've got a nice little job if you want it.'

He had such a disarming way about him I agreed to go with him without thinking, my powers of judgement no doubt befuddled by a mixture of drugs and hunger. As he led me down onto a tube train the fears were already starting to take root inside me. What was I doing? I was in a strange city and I knew nothing about this guy. Why had I agreed to go with him? But by then I was too scared to say anything or make a run for it, so I just sat silently beside him in the loud, rattling carriage, waiting stupidly to see what would happen next. I was no more than a defenceless, lost child. I had no idea where we were going or how I would get back and I had no money at all. I had put myself completely at the mercy of a man who made his living from pimping. His mood had changed now we were down in the tunnels of the underground and he was talking to me in an aggressive tone, all his smiley street charm evaporating as if I had irritated it out of him, as if I was a burden to him with my childish nervousness.

'Where are we going?' I asked.

'Shut the fuck up,' he snapped. 'You'll fucking see when we get there.'

I felt a prick in my arm on the side where he was sitting but by the time I looked down there was nothing there. Looking back I'm pretty sure he injected me with something, but at the time I couldn't work out what had happened and my mind was beginning to cloud over even more. I suddenly felt really stoned and couldn't concentrate at all on what was going on around me, like I was dreaming the whole scene. A little part of my brain told me that I was going to die, but I couldn't do anything about it. I could do nothing but submit to this man's guiding hands as he bundled me roughly out of the carriage at our destination. All I wanted to do was lie down and sleep but he kept propelling me forward, catching me and propping me back up impatiently whenever I stumbled. There was no way now that my legs would have been able to run even if I'd had the courage to try. It was taking every ounce of my concentration just to walk and I wouldn't have known where to run to anyway.

As we emerged into the light I couldn't see any white faces in any direction. This was a world he was comfortable in and I felt very alone and very vulnerable. He led me along roads filled with identical-looking little houses.

I could hear reggae music playing and the atmosphere was relaxed and friendly and hippyish. I was aware of the aromas of unfamiliar foods. When we went into one of the houses there seemed to be people everywhere, and I think there was a party going on. My escort gripped my arm hard, pushed me down firmly onto a settee and left me as the party went on around me in a dizzying sway of strange faces and voices, none of which I could quite get into focus. Despite all the fears clamouring to make themselves heard in my fuzzy head I was unable to stop myself from giving in to the overwhelming need to sleep.

When I woke up it was five or six o'clock in the morning. The room swam into focus around me as I strained to remember where I was and how I had got there. All about me were sleeping bodies but I couldn't see the pimp from King's Cross anywhere. I felt a rush of relief to find that I was still alive and apparently unharmed. Being careful not to disturb anyone I gingerly got to my feet and tiptoed out of the house, quietly pulling the front door behind me and walking away in the dawn light, not having any idea where I was going but wanting to put as much distance between me and that house as possible.

However hard I tried to concentrate I couldn't work out what might have happened during the hours that I was sleeping in that house, but I was deeply grateful to be alive. Had I been raped, perhaps by more than one man? Or did they just leave me alone since I was so soundly asleep? God knows how I managed it with no money – I must have begged a tube fare off someone or jumped the barriers – but I got back to the squat where Brian was almost at the point of contacting the police to report me missing. He was beside himself with worry and I was deeply shaken to think how much danger I had put myself in. I could so easily have disappeared that night, never to be seen again, and I doubt if the police would have put in too much time looking for me.

The whole London experience was making me a nervous wreck. I felt almost as insecure and threatened inside the squat as I did out on the streets. A Scottish couple lived on the floor above us, both of them heavy drinkers who would row in voices filled with bitterness and aggression whenever they were drunk. It sounded as though they had a long history of grievances, which the drink released over and over again. During one of their endless fights the man finally lost his grip on reality and stabbed his partner in the stomach on the stairs just outside our room. There was blood everywhere and I was terrified that sooner or later Brian and I were going to end up murdered in our beds.

We decided it was time to admit we'd made a mistake and to leave London before anything worse happened. We got back onto the road out of the city and headed up to Northampton to stay with another friend of Brian's called Kevin.

Chapter Eighteen

facing the music

Kevin lived on his own, apart from a black Labrador called Fish, in a little cottage a couple of miles from the Santa Pod raceway, which is a famous drag-racing venue. Tina, one of the prostitutes who had been in the flat the first night I met Brian, came up too and we would all go to the drag racing together, mixing and drinking with people who had travelled from all over the country to spend their weekends up there in tents. It was exciting to be part of their community amongst the good-natured motor enthusiasts, hanging out in the ear-shattering roar of the cars and the fog of exhaust fumes. I was hugely relieved to have got away from the aggression and danger of the streets in King's Cross to a place of relative safety. Here we could relax and breathe again and be more ourselves.

We had only been away from Norwich for six weeks

but it was long enough for my picture to have been published in the local papers with a story explaining that I had disappeared and asking the public for any information they might have about my whereabouts. The information they had put out about me wasn't exactly flattering. They said I was 'about 5 ft 6 in tall, has short auburn hair, a slightly spotty complexion and sometimes wears glasses. She is quite stocky and looks older than 15.' The description fulfilled all my worst fears about myself. Dad's words rang in my ears: 'You're fat and ugly and no one but me will ever love you.' But Brian did love me, of that I was sure, and that was the best feeling I had ever experienced.

Although we frequently had no money at all during those weeks, we weren't completely reliant on my earnings because Brian had his benefits; they just weren't nearly enough to support us and our various drug and alcohol habits. Once a fortnight during the time we were in London, Brian had hitchhiked back to Norwich to sign on the dole and get his money, which meant I was on my own for two or three days while he waited for the money to come through. I never liked it when he was away, feeling vulnerable and lost, but I knew he had to go. He did the same from Northampton, but this time the police were waiting for him at the dole office and he was arrested when he got there. They grabbed him and demanded to know where he had hidden me.

Tina phoned from Norwich to tell me what had happened and I knew the game was up. I was really upset that just when I was beginning to feel settled it all went wrong again. Realizing I needed a friend, Tina travelled back to Northampton to fetch me and Dick-the-Shit. I wanted to come back to Norwich myself in order to explain to the authorities that Brian was completely innocent, that far from abducting me he had actually been helping me to escape from Dad, who was the real villain of the story. Tina was still living at the flat in Norwich so once we got back to the city she took over looking after Dick and I surrendered myself to the social services.

The social workers knew pretty much everything there was to know about me by then. They knew about me being on the game, and they all knew that Dad had abused me, even though they hadn't yet got round to pressing charges against him. Now they had Brian in their clutches they finally seemed to think they had enough to go on and both he and Dad were charged with living off my immoral earnings. My world came crashing round my ears; this was the last thing I'd ever wanted to happen.

It tore me in two when I had to go into court to give evidence against Dad. I stood in the witness box for about an hour and a half with him staring long and hard at me, and there were so many emotions flooding through me. I hated him and loved him at the same time; I was pleased that people now believed me and that he was finally going to pay for what he had done to me over the years but I also felt guilty that I was betraying him and ensuring that he went back to prison yet again.

To make me feel a thousand times worse my grandmother was waiting for me outside the courtroom, screaming abuse at me, telling me what a liar and a bitch I was for saying these things about her precious son Terry, not caring who heard her ranting or what they thought of us.

'How can you do this to my son?' she yelled. 'To your own father? He would never do those things to you! Why are you telling all these lies?'

The court disagreed with her. They didn't think I was a liar. They believed every word of it. Dad was found guilty and was sentenced to four years. The judge made a point of saying it was the maximum sentence he could give for the offence as he knew the whole story and wanted to reflect the public revulsion at how Dad had behaved towards me over the years. The fact that he was my father and that I was underage made Dad's crimes all the more repellent and unacceptable to everyone who heard about them, including other prisoners he was likely to meet once he was inside. Child abusers don't get treated well in places like prison.

I heard later that he was taken to one of the special units where they put nonces and rapists and other sex

offenders for their own protection. I used to hear sometimes of the things the other inmates do to sex offenders,
like giving them humiliating haircuts or uniforms that
don't fit with trousers halfway up their ankles. They
would put bits of glass in their food and chuck slops down
onto their landing so they would get covered in it. I have
to admit there was a part of me that liked the idea that
other people were taking revenge on my behalf, sticking
up for me, confirming that what Dad had done to me was
wrong, just as I had always believed it was. Such humili-
ation would be even worse for someone who was as vain
and pleased with himself as Dad was. He liked to be
admired by those around him, not despised.

At the same time I feared for him and his tendency to
depression. Even in my moments of vindication part of
me still felt guilty and worried about what I had done to
him. I knew that a lot of men ended up driven to suicide
when they found themselves in positions like his and Dad
had shown many times that he was capable of such acts of
self-destruction when he was low.

Having to give evidence in court against Brian, the
man I loved and who had proved in so many ways that he
loved me, was even harder. They tried to convict him for
abducting me, but I stuck up for him so vehemently they
couldn't make that charge stick. Being an inherently hon-
est man, however, he couldn't deny that he'd had sex with
me or that he had shared the money I earned in London

in order to eat, so he was given six months for having sex with a minor and for living off my immoral earnings.

It all came as a bit of a shock to Brian, who hadn't really thought he was doing anything wrong. I suspect he had grown so used to treating me like I was the same age as him and the rest of his friends that he had pretty much forgotten I was officially still a child during our time together. He even talked about suing the police for wrongful arrest before the gravity of his situation was explained to him clearly by his lawyers.

It was obvious that the courts had to be seen to do something about what had happened, but any attempt by the prosecution to make Brian sound like a paedophile rang very hollow. He was indisputably my boyfriend and even though I was underage I had been sleeping with men for money for over two years by then, so I was hardly your average innocent little schoolgirl. What he had done was more of a technical misdemeanour than a great moral crime. The length of his sentence compared to the one handed down to Dad showed that the judge did not view their crimes in the same light, but that he couldn't turn a blind eye completely to what Brian had done. The judge made it clear that I had consented to the sex with Brian, which I had never done with Dad, and the newspaper coverage of the case reflected that sympathetically. However, I still felt guilty about the catastrophic effect I'd had on his life, and I missed him terribly.

Like Dad, when he went into prison Brian was offered the sort of protection that paedophiles and sex offenders can have, but he categorically refused to accept it. He wanted to be treated like every other prisoner because he wasn't ashamed of anything he had done. Everyone in the prison would have known the story by the time he got there, and would have known about Dad. Like me they would have seen Brian more as a hero for trying to get me away from Dad than as the villain of the story. No one gave him any trouble and he settled into prison life as philosophically as he settled into everything else. Brian was such a sweet-natured man he never once blamed me for his predicament, just shrugged and got on with serving his time, looking forward to our future together once he was out and once I was old enough to live with him openly.

In the meantime the authorities had to think what to do with me and I was sent back to Bramerton. I was heartbroken that they had taken Brian away because he had such a calming influence on me and at that age a six-month sentence seemed like a lifetime, but at least now I believed I could envisage a future for myself, a future with him. I'm sure the authorities thought our great love affair would peter out while we were apart, that there would be no chance someone with my past record would wait six months for any man, but they were wrong. For the first time in my life I had someone who cared about me, someone who was willing to put his neck on the block and go to prison for me and I wasn't about to throw that away.

As the months passed and they saw that we were still writing to one another all the time and that I wasn't going off with any other men, the staff at Bramerton began to realize that we weren't going to be so easily separated and they allowed me to go to visit him in prison. It wasn't depressing or frightening, like visiting Dad had been all those years before when Terry and I were kids. It was lovely to see him, even though we had to have a social worker sitting with us all through the visit. He was still his same easygoing self, just accepting the way things were without bitterness and saying nice things to me, making me feel special.

The prison governor and Mrs Mcquarrie at Bramerton used to talk to one another on the phone and between them they came to the conclusion that Brian actually might be quite good for me. He was the opposite of Dad in every way, always advising me not to run away from Bramerton and not to go on the game, assuring me we were going to get married and be all right as soon as he had served his time and I was old enough. They started to find ways of letting us talk to one another on the phone. The governor would arrange to get Brian into his office and would ring Mrs Mcquarrie who would then call me into her office and hand me the phone.

Despite Brian's calming words, however, it wasn't long before I was escaping again. The habit was just too deeply ingrained in me to stop. Most of the time I didn't even know why I did it, any more than I knew why I smoked cigarettes, took drugs or drank. Maybe it was the challenge each time because Bramerton wasn't that easy to get out of. There was only one lane in and out so I couldn't use that if I wanted to run away as it would be the first place they would go looking, so I always had to start out across the fields, hiding behind the hedges and trees, which was bloody hard work. I would start out quite fast, pumped up with adrenaline, but I soon got tired and wished I had never bothered. It reminded me of the horrors of cross-country running, which Wymondham College used to make us do and which used to nearly kill me.

On one of these escapes I finally staggered out onto the main road at a point I thought would be safe at about nine at night. Having picked off the various bits of hedge and kicked the worst of the mud from my boots I stuck my thumb out for a lift into Norwich. It wasn't long before a car drew up and the smart-looking man at the wheel said he would take me. I climbed in gratefully.

'What are you doing out at this time of night?' he asked as we drove off.

'I've just been round my friend's house to do my homework,' I told him. 'I've missed my last bus home and my dad's going to kill me if I'm late.'

'Don't worry,' he said, 'we'll soon get you there nice and safe. You don't have to worry about anything. I'm a policeman.'

I don't know if blood actually can run cold, but it certainly felt like mine did at that moment. I was sure I was about to be driven straight back to Bramerton. Trying not to show my shock I kept the pretence going, hoping I might be able to bluff my way through. He was very friendly and tried asking me a few questions, which I lied my way out of quite easily.

'Where are your books for homework then?' he asked after a while.

'Oh, you know what they're like,' I said airily, 'all those bloody textbooks. My friend gets a lift in with her parents so she's taking mine in for me to save me carrying them.'

'You're not one of those runaways from Bramerton, are you?' he joked at one stage.

'Excuse me?' I hoped I wasn't blushing. 'What's Bramerton?'

'Haven't you heard of it?' He laughed. 'That big children's home over the fields.'

'What sort of people go there then?' I asked and he rabbited happily on for the rest of the journey. I guess he thought I was much older than I was, and dismissed the idea of me being a Bramerton girl as ridiculous. He dropped me off in town without showing the slightest flicker of suspicion and then drove on to the police station to start his next shift, probably feeling pleased with himself for being such a chivalrous knight of the road. I later heard that when he got there he looked at the log to see what was going on and only then realized who I must be. When I was eventually picked up and taken back, the staff at Bramerton told me how furious he was.

'God help you if you ever meet him again,' they laughed. 'He was really mad.'

Even though I carried on running away from Bramerton while Brian and Dad were both in jail, I always stayed completely faithful to Brian, waiting for him to come out so we could start our lives together properly. I used to get drunk and high a lot in order to try to forget how lost and lonely and confused I felt but I stayed off the game. A lot of the boys at Bramerton tried to chat me up and I used to play pool with them and everything, but I was never tempted to stray; they were just mates. I was in love with a grown-up man.

With Dad out of the way, Kathy really wanted to help and agreed to have me to stay with her so that I could get out of care for a bit and try to adapt to normal everyday life. She is such a sweet woman and she gave me a nice room of my own in her house on the condition that I behaved and got in by a certain time every night. I wanted to please her but I was back to socializing with a lot of the working girls I had known when I was on the street and I would go to the same pub as them, the Brown Derby, most nights, even running my own slate there. My drinking was getting way out of control and one night I drank fourteen pints of Snakebite (a mixture of cider and lager) in the space of a few hours. There was one particular hooker there called Sally, a great big scary-looking woman who'd recently had her nose pierced. I was terrified of her but I was never going to let her know that.

'I'd like to do that,' I said, tapping the side of my nose.

'I'll do it for you,' she offered.

There was no backing down now. I had to let her know I was as tough as her or I would never hear the end of it.

'Sure,' I said bravely, like it was the most normal thing in the world.

'Come on then.'

We wove our way to the ladies' toilet and she jabbed a stud into my nose, pushing it straight through. It really, really hurt but I wasn't going to let on. My eyes were streaming but I held in the cries, just as I used to when Dad was beating me. He had trained me well for situations like that. I kept the stud in and amazingly it never even went septic.

In the end Kathy couldn't take the worry of being responsible for me. She would try to reason with me every time I rolled in drunk and high in the early hours of the morning, and I would feel really remorseful about letting her down again once I had sobered up. I would apologize and promise to be good, but then I would get bored or blue and I would be off again. I really wanted to please her but it was as if I was on a direct course of self-destruction. I knew it wasn't fair to ask her to put up with me any longer and I went back to Bramerton without making any fuss, knowing that it was now only a few more weeks before Brian would be out of prison and we could be together.

By that stage most of the staff at Bramerton were used to me and knew how to handle me. Sometimes after I had been on the run for a while I would just give up and ring them and ask someone to come and get me. Once, after the pubs were closed, I was so drunk that I threw up all over the car that came to fetch me. I must have stretched their patience to the absolute limit but they had pretty much given up trying to tell me what to do and what not to do and they would laugh at me instead.

'Why did you do that then?' they would ask every time I did something stupid. 'When are you going to be going on the run again then?'

They were endlessly patient because I was always letting them down. I would take whatever punishment they doled out for a few weeks – such as extra chores or withdrawn privileges. I'd earn their trust back and then throw it all away again on a stupid whim. Maybe they just thought I was a lost cause.

Chapter Nineteen

falling pregnant

My sixteenth birthday came and went, Brian was released from jail and there was no stopping me. Nothing was going to keep me apart from him for long. I would run away to see him at every opportunity, just as I had previously run away to see Dad. The staff at Bramerton decided to let me visit him at weekends, willing to accept that we were in a proper relationship now that I had passed sixteen and become legal. We were really in love.

As soon as I discovered I'd fallen pregnant I knew exactly when it had happened. The first time Brian had come to visit me at Bramerton after he was released we had gone for a walk together. He'd been inside for all those months so it wasn't surprising that we were both keen to make love. We didn't bother with precautions because I really wanted to get pregnant with Brian as the father, so I was delighted when I found out the plan had worked first time. It wasn't long, however, before other people started to undermine my joy and make me wonder if I had done the wrong thing.

'The best thing you can do for that child,' one of the less sympathetic staff at Bramerton told me, cruelly puncturing my bubble, 'is to have an abortion. You'll always be an unfit mother and that baby's life will be a nightmare.'

I'd had it fixed in my mind for over a year that I wanted a baby, something all of my own, someone to care for and nurture and be responsible for. And Brian was keen too, not having managed to have a child in his previous relationships. I thought that if I had a baby it would give me a focus in life but now this woman was putting doubts into my head. I had thought that perhaps a baby would save me from the temptation to fall back into prostitution when I was next desperate for money. It seemed like my best chance of leading a decent independent life, but maybe she was right and it would be unfair for someone as worthless as me to bring a child into the world. It didn't take much to re-ignite all my insecurities about myself.

Another reason I had wanted to fall pregnant was because I'd read somewhere that girls who have been abused when they are very young can sometimes be so physically damaged inside that they are never able to conceive and I wanted to reassure myself that that wasn't the case for me. But now the seeds of doubt had been sown all my old feelings of inferiority came bubbling back to the surface. What, I asked myself, made me think that someone as bad as me deserved to have a baby? I decided the woman must be right, that it would be the kindest thing if I had an abortion rather than condemn my child to a childhood as miserable as mine.

I went to see Mrs Mcquarrie and the matron and told them that I had decided to get rid of the baby. They listened to what I was saying but Mrs Mcquarrie seemed to be really off with me, which was a shock as I had expected her to be supportive of my decision and her opinion meant a lot to me.

My social worker, who thought I should have an abortion, escorted me to the doctor to get him to make the necessary referral.

'Can you tell me why you want this abortion?' the doctor asked me, pointedly not looking at the social worker as he talked.

'Because everyone has told me that I can't have a child because I'm useless and because of my lifestyle,' I said matter-of-factly.

'But what do you really want?' he asked.

I burst into tears. 'I want this baby.'

'Well,' he said, sitting back in his chair, 'there's no way I'm going to recommend that you have an abortion when it's not what you want.'

It was like he had lifted a huge weight off my heart. I was delighted that someone was actually listening to what I wanted rather than telling me what they thought I should do. From that moment on there was no chance I was going to get rid of that baby. I left the surgery unable to wipe the broad grin off my face, ignoring my social worker's mutterings and grumblings. Once we got back to Bramerton I went straight in to see Mrs Mcquarrie.

'I'm not having an abortion now,' I said.

'Well, I should bloody well think not,' she replied.

'Is that why you've been off with me?'

'Yes. You're a perfectly healthy young woman who got pregnant on purpose, so why would you then decide to get rid of it?'

'It was because of what the others said.'

'Well, bugger them.' She grinned. 'We're having a baby, so let's get on with it.'

Once the staff realized that I was going to become a mother they weren't sure what to do with me next. By that stage I was refusing point blank to go into school so I spent more and more time with Mrs Mcquarrie or with the staff and I happily set about knitting cardigans, bonnets and booties.

Over the years that I had been at Bramerton I had eventually formed good relationships with a number of staff members, even though it didn't start out that way. The people I got on best with were the domestic staff and I spent most of my time in the kitchens with them. The housekeeper, Renee, and the chef were both great to me and I learnt more from them than I had ever learnt from the teacher in the school. I would never talk to Renee about any of my emotional or mental problems, which was a relief: her mission in life was to do with practical things, like cooking and baking and making sure everyone was warm and clean and well fed. A lot of the boys, many of whom were pretty hard cases and not long away from prison, found the same with the gardener, who used to take them outside to work with him in the vegetable patch. In the last year or so of my time there the domestic staff actually became like my surrogate family.

If I wasn't going to go to the school any more they said I had to go out and get a job, which seemed like a completely foreign concept to me. I'd never really known anyone who had a normal job, and whenever people asked me what I wanted to do when I grew up all I could ever think to say was, 'I want to get married and have four children.' Now that they were insisting that I came up with an alternative career plan I shrugged and said, 'Work in a shop?' I couldn't think of anything else.

'But you're an intelligent girl,' they protested. 'Don't you want to do more than that with your life? You could go to college, get some qualifications and have a career.'

I didn't really think I was good enough for anything else, because that was what Dad had always drummed into me, but as they were now insisting I come up with something I admitted I had enjoyed working with the disabled children in Break. Clutching at this straw, they arranged for me to go to work in a local home for the disabled, a position that allowed me to live in a sort of supervised flat on my own. I could still see Brian when I wanted to, so I felt quite pleased with myself. Maybe my life wasn't going to be quite such a complete failure as I had been anticipating.

One morning a few weeks later I woke up with terrible pains and bleeding. The doctor was called and said I must stay in bed and they should call an ambulance if the bleeding got any heavier. By lunchtime it was getting much worse and an ambulance was summoned. I was petrified. Mrs Mcquarrie dashed over to be with me and she seemed almost as frightened and worried as I was and insisted on coming with me herself. She held my hand on the way to the hospital, which meant a lot to me. She was still there as they wheeled me off into the operating theatre and the first thing I saw when I opened my eyes was her concerned face looking down at me.

'Have I lost my baby?' I asked, and the answer was written all over her face.

'Yes,' she nodded. 'I'm so sorry.'

I was devastated and wept for days and weeks on end. To be given something you want so much, something as wonderful as a pregnancy, and then have it snatched away again without warning, just felt unbearable. Brian was really cut up as well, but at least I knew now that I could get pregnant and I was clear in my mind that I wanted a baby of my own. I was determined to try again at the first opportunity.

Chapter Twenty

entering the outside world

By the age of seventeen I was still an uncomfortable mixture of maturity and immaturity. Social services felt they had done all they could for me and there wasn't much point in keeping me in care till I was eighteen, or a ward of court till I was twenty-one, just for the sake of it. As they knew I was going to be constantly running away from any institution they tried to put me in, they decided to let me go officially to see if that would work and if I would be capable of taking responsibility for my own life. The same judge who had sentenced Brian to six months lifted the care order on me, and the ward of court order, and sent me off to live with him. Less than a year earlier they had been telling me to stay away from him because he was dangerous, and now they were wishing us well and telling us to live happily ever after. I guess it was good that they were prepared to be flexible and to see that my needs were changing, but actually I was no more equipped for dealing with the real world than poor old Brian was.

In my youthful arrogance I was certain I knew what I was doing and I basically told social services I didn't need their help any more because I had a man to look after me – my man. They must have been relieved to see the back of me although I wonder if they ever really believed we had any chance of making it, especially if I was planning to have a baby. It was probably obvious to everyone but me that Brian was not going to find the responsibilities of fatherhood easy, but when you are young and know nothing you think you can do anything you want as long as other people just stop interfering.

Brian got a council flat, I moved in with him and I fell pregnant again almost immediately. I was ecstatic to be having another chance at a baby, but it wasn't long before I began to worry that maybe Brian wasn't going to be the most reliable family provider. When it was just him and me to think about and provide for it hadn't been so important because I always knew I could go out and earn a few pounds on the game if I had to, even if I didn't want to. But there was no way I was going to be doing that while I was carrying my precious baby and that made me feel vulnerable.

Although Brian did get a job as a decorator, he was already in debt to the council for not paying his rent, having preferred to spend all his money on drink and drugs.

His drinking was getting much worse, soaking up every penny he earned, just as Dad's had. The gas had been disconnected and the electricity supplier had installed a meter because of the problem with unpaid bills. Without gas I had to boil water in saucepans and kettles if I wanted to take a bath, which made everything a hundred times more difficult.

Quite often we would run out of coins for the meter halfway through the week and I would have to sit alone in the dark and the cold until Brian was paid at the end of the week. Even when he was paid he would stop off at the pub on the way home and spend most of his earnings. I couldn't get my head round the thought of getting some dead-end job myself and Brian took exception to having to support me just to sit around at home. He told me I had to contribute to the household budget if I wanted food and I knew he was right. I just couldn't muster the strength to get out there and do something about it. I must have been really winding him up because when he'd had a few drinks he started to get a bit violent with me, something that he would never have done in the past.

Although I was obsessed with my baby I didn't have much ready for the birth, not even a bottle or a babygro, and I was becoming increasingly worried about how I was ever going to manage to get all the things I needed. I had been so excited at the prospect of having a baby of my own that I had been letting it blind me to the reality of the situation, but gradually it was dawning on me that we both had to get our acts together. Whenever I felt panicked I would start going on at Brian again, putting pressure on him to get all the things I needed. Rather than being the cheerful, carefree fellow traveller that he had fallen in love with I must have been beginning to seem like a burden to him and a handicap to his previously freewheeling hippy-like existence. Before I got pregnant we had been two irresponsible children together, but now at least one of us was going to have to grow up quickly.

'Get a job,' he said when I protested that I had no money for all the things I needed.

'Like what?' I challenged him.

'I don't know,' he shrugged. 'Get a paper round or something.'

I could see that he had a point but my confidence had sunk to an all-time low and I don't think anyone would have given me a job even if I could have plucked up the courage and energy to go asking for one. All I cared about was my baby but I wasn't making any sensible decisions about that either, just worrying and panicking all the time. I know I became a permanent nag to Brian, always going on at him about the eviction letters that kept arriving from the council and wondering out loud what would become of me and my baby if we were made homeless and thrown out onto the street. I could envisage the two of us huddled in some doorway, begging for spare change or, worse still, social services taking the baby away from me and giving it to someone who was doing a better job of getting their life in order.

I could see that Brian had gone too far off the rails to be able to be a support for me and although I still loved him I was coming to realize that he was unlikely to be able to turn his life round now, certainly not in time for the baby's arrival, but I didn't know what to do about it or who to turn to for help. I could hardly go back to Mum after being rebuffed so many times, and even if Dad had provided any sort of option he was still in prison.

By the time the council eventually evicted Brian from the flat I was six or seven months pregnant and winter was approaching. I hadn't been eating properly for weeks and I fainted one day on the bus into the city. I wanted so much to be a great mother but already I knew I wasn't doing my baby any favours by becoming so stressed and run down. The more I worried about it the worse the situation got.

As my delivery date drew closer I had to accept that being independent wasn't going to work. I was going to have to face the fact that I couldn't cope and throw myself on the mercy of others. I felt like a complete failure. With a heavy heart but unable to see any other way forward, I left Brian and made myself homeless. I hated the idea of social services seeing me as a failure again and I was terri-fied they would insist on taking my baby away from me but in the end I realized I was more frightened that I was putting my baby's life in danger than anything else and I plucked up the courage to go to them. Having boasted to them a few months before that I could manage without them I had to slink back with my tail between my legs and admit that I needed their help.

They responded to my pleas graciously, probably not very surprised to find me back on their doorstep, and put me into a women's refuge called Little Portion while they looked for other accommodation for me. It was ironic, but probably not surprising, that I should end up in the same home where my mother had been years before.

Little Portion was run by nuns and I would love to be able to say that it was a sympathetic, caring environment but it wasn't. Maybe it was my own sense of feeling like a useless failure that prejudiced their opinion of me but I was certainly made to feel like a scarlet woman. It was a very strict regime. No men were allowed, which was obviously a good thing, and we had to be in bed at certain times. The food was sparse and the whole environment was stifled, cold and intimidating. The nuns were never openly unkind to us but it was not a warm, supportive experience.

While I was there I met a girl called Lisa who had a small child called Jessica and we became friends. Social services found me my own flat shortly before the baby was due, and I moved in and spent Christmas there on my own before I managed to persuade Lisa to come and share with me, bringing Jessica too. This meant I didn't have to face the approaching birth on my own and I had someone there to give me moral support whenever I felt panicky. Social services didn't like the idea, saying Lisa was trouble because she had a violent ex-boyfriend, but I really liked her and it gave me company at a time when I was feeling very alone and low.

By this stage I felt I had lost my whole family. Dad was still in jail but anyway he was so pissed off with me for going off with Brian that he had let me know he wanted nothing more to do with me, and I felt a real sense of loss about that despite everything we'd been through. I hardly ever got to see Terry any more and Chris and Glen were leading completely separate lives and I wasn't allowed to make contact with them. I didn't want my baby to come into the world with no relatives at all so I wrote to Mum, resenting the fact that yet again it was me who was making the effort to make contact and not her, to tell her she was going to be a grandmother. I asked her if she wanted to get in touch, and to my surprise she did. We saw each other a couple of times, trying our best to repair our poor relationship. She was with a new man by then, who had taken on my new baby half-brother, Adam, as his own. Although he had been willing to do that he made it clear there was no way he was willing to take on any of her four other children. He said that she could speak to us on the phone and we could go round to see her when he was out at work, but he didn't want anything to do with us himself. Given our history I suppose I can understand his attitude although it could hardly have been described as charitable, either to us or to Mum and Adam.

Brian came to the hospital to be with me during the birth, although I later found out that the night before he had been out with another woman, not in a restaurant with friends as he had told me. He was completely drunk when he arrived and fell fast asleep in the waiting room, which didn't exactly show him up in a good light. The nurse had to wake him up to tell him his baby was on the way. Once I was in labour I lost interest in such petty matters. Everything that was happening in that delivery room was between me and my new baby boy. This was my chance to start all over again with a new life to care for.

He was just gorgeous when he came out. I didn't sleep at all during the first night after the birth, just lying there staring at him, marvelling at how tiny and perfect he was, talking to him, promising that I would do everything I possibly could to give him a decent life and that I would make sure he didn't have to endure the sort of upbringing I'd been given. It was love at first sight and I was overwhelmed with the strength of the emotion I felt for this little creature. I called him Brendan after a lovely bloke I'd worked with in the disabled home – a big, ginger-haired, freckled Irish chap who had a real presence and who had been a good friend to me during the time I worked there.

One of the first people to come and visit Brendan and me in hospital was Mrs Mcquarrie, along with Renee, the housekeeper from Bramerton. Kathy came too, bringing all sorts of bits and pieces that I needed. Brian arrived with a big bouquet of flowers and a card signed by everyone at the pub, making me feel like I belonged to a little community, even if they were a pretty hopeless bunch of deadbeats. Even Brian's mum and sister came to see us.

When I'd recovered from the birth, they sent me to a mother and baby unit for ten days so they could teach me everything they thought I needed to know about looking after him. I was determined to be the best mother I could but I struggled terribly for the first few days. I was trying to breastfeed him but it was so painful I would cry sometimes, although I wouldn't give up. Eventually it became easier and I had so much milk that the midwives suggested I expressed some to be used for the tiny babies in the special care unit. I also remember them giving Brendan an injection in his heel and I couldn't stay in the room when I heard his screams. Every instinct in me wanted to protect him and shield him from pain.

Lisa gave me a book on childrearing by Miriam Stoppard, which became my bible as I struggled to get everything exactly right for him. I went to a few parentcraft classes to try to learn more but all the other mothers were there with their husbands or partners and I felt embarrassed that I was having to attend on my own.

The day Brendan was born, when I was eighteen years old, my life changed and everything that happened from then on was no longer about me. It was the day I grew up. Having a new baby of my own made me remember Chris and Glen and the way they were treated in their early years. Mum and Dad's neglect of them seemed even more incomprehensible to me now that I was a mother myself than it had at the time. Every natural instinct I possessed made me want to protect my child, no matter where he had come from or who his father might be. I couldn't understand how my parents had been able to treat their own children the way they had.

By the time I was allowed to take Brendan back to the flat, Lisa and Jessica had already moved on but Brian started coming round to visit, saying he wanted to spend time with us. A few weeks before I would have been touched by that, but now I had a responsibility, a new focus for my life. I knew I had to be practical and I realized that Brian was just sponging off me, eating my food, soaking up money that should have been used to buy things for Brendan. He didn't provide anything – all I possessed was the bits and pieces that other people were giving me – and I knew I had to move on with my life. But at least he was a friendly face and a bit of adult company now and again, even if he was usually high or drunk when he turned up at the door.

All the reports from Doris, the social worker who was handling my case by then, bear out how completely Brendan changed my behaviour. She wrote glowingly about how I was coping and what a brilliant mother I was. Reading her notes now it's like she was writing about a completely different person to the one described in all the previous social services reports, but in reality I was still the same worried little girl who didn't think she was good enough for anything. I was struggling to stay afloat. I started shoplifting clothes for Brendan because I couldn't bear for him to have to go without and I was spending almost all my benefits on fuel in order to keep the flat warm enough for him.

I didn't have a washing machine or a spin dryer and although many people were using disposable nappies at the time I would use the terry towelling ones to save money. I would have to hand wash them every day and the smell of urine plus the wet nappies hanging around the flat contributed to the cold and damp, and to my growing feelings of misery and despair. At one stage the midwife gave me a real dressing down for not having the temperature high enough for a baby and it broke my heart to think I was trying so hard and still wasn't able to give Brendan the most basic things that he needed. I remembered how cold it had been in our house when we were children and I didn't want my baby to have to suffer anything like that.

Doris was a great woman but a visit from her for half an hour a week wasn't really going to solve my problems or change anything fundamental. For most of the time it was just me and the baby in the flat. I didn't have any days or nights of my own; every hour was dedicated to looking after Brendan and catering for his needs.

Doris knew I was struggling because she even brought me some coal round to help keep the fire going, but I didn't want her to know exactly how hard I was finding it to cope in case she decided Brendan would be better off with someone else.

I wanted to do everything right but I didn't know how. I had never seen my mother cooking or keeping the house clean and she wasn't around enough to ask now. I was having to learn everything from scratch. I'd buy a bottle of bleach to clean the toilet but I would have no idea how often I was meant to do it or how much bleach I was meant to use. I was like an alien suddenly landing in a domestic situation and having to work everything out for myself.

I kept hearing how people who had been abused as children ended up as abusers themselves. I felt no urge to abuse Brendan in any way – I just wanted to look after him and protect him – but I was terrified some force hidden deep inside me would fight its way to the surface and turn me into a monster like my father. A hundred different questions were going through my head. At what age should I stop getting in the bath with him? When should I stop walking about the house in front of him in my underwear? I was terrified of getting it wrong, of being like Dad. Sometimes I was even scared to cuddle him. I had no idea where the boundaries should be.

The need for money preyed on my mind twenty-four hours a day, but I didn't want to get a full-time job because I didn't want to be away from Brendan and I couldn't afford childminders anyway. I hated the idea of stealing and didn't want to risk getting caught and giving them an excuse to take Brendan into care. There had only ever been one way that I had known to make easy money, so when Brendan was six months old I summoned all the courage I could find and went back out on the game to try to get some quick cash to buy us a few of the things we needed.

I took Brendan round to Lisa's new place and asked her to look after him for a couple of hours, not telling her what I was doing, not telling anyone, knowing that it was a terrible decision even as I made it. I knew that if I was seen by anyone from social services they would almost certainly take Brendan away from me. It was a giant backward step and I felt like the lowest of the low as I climbed into those men's cars.

I only did it twice and I knew as I was doing it that it was all wrong, that I was going to have to find another way to survive. I felt so guilty about breaking the promise I'd made to Brendan on his first night in the world that I would give him a decent life. I knew from experience that the money I was making from those punters wasn't going to last more than a couple of days and if I followed this road I was going to be back on the street full time by the end of the week. How long would it be before I was arrested or beaten up by a punter, rolling home to my baby with blackened eyes and broken teeth? I remembered all the nights that Lucy had ended up on our doorstep, battered and bruised. I knew her daughter was now following in her footsteps but I had to break the cycle if I wanted any chance of giving Brendan something better than I'd had myself. I knew that I was failing but I didn't know what to do about it.

I used to take Brendan out in the pram for really long walks during the day, pushing him for miles and miles, to get us both out of the flat and to give myself some space to think. Although I loved Brendan more than anything I had ever loved before, a dark cloud of despair was gathering around me. In my attempts to escape from it I had started drinking heavily at home, sometimes getting through a bottle of vodka a day as I plodded through my solitary routines. In my blackest moments I wondered if maybe the woman at Bramerton had been right after all when she said I would be incapable of bringing up a baby and that he was bound to have a miserable childhood.

What sort of life could he hope to have with a mother who couldn't do anything except drink all day and sell her body to pay for it? I was terrified I would end up just like Mum, separated from my children, or dead and mutilated in some bushes somewhere. On her fleeting visits Doris was talking about sending me to psychology groups to try to help me come to terms with my past. She introduced me to a woman who did a lot of fostering who she thought might be able to help me by babysitting for Brendan sometimes, giving me a bit of a chance to make a life for myself.

When Brendan was around eight months old I met a very successful businessman called David, who was incredibly supportive and helpful. Although I had an enormous crush on him, he was never interested in me in any romantic or sexual way. He had just separated from his wife and was definitely anti-women for a while. David genuinely wanted to help me and offered me a job answering his telephone whilst he was out working. I was able to take Brendan with me. As well as answering the phone and doing basic secretarial duties, I would do some housework for him as well. David was really pleased with me. He wasn't able to pay me much money because I was receiving benefits but with the little he was able to give me I started taking driving lessons. It was a good feeling to be doing something respectable. This was clean, decent money that I had earned legitimately and honestly, which was why it felt so different, and I was determined to use it in a respectful way.

One day as I was walking back home from David's a truckload of lads drew up beside me, whistling and cat calling.

'Do you want a lift home?' one of them shouted out the van window.

'No,' I said, 'I'm all right. I'm walking the baby.'

'Give us your phone number then,' he said.

He was a big, stocky man in his late twenties and I rather liked the look of him so I gave him my number but when I didn't hear anything from him during the following days I thought no more about it. I had enough on my mind without worrying about men.

Despite the job working for David, I couldn't raise any optimism about the future. I still felt a terrible weight of depression and worry at the sort of life I was going to be able to give Brendan, whatever choices I made. Added to this, I heard that Dad was about to be released from jail, after serving most of his four-year sentence, and I was very apprehensive about what it would be like to see him again. One day I reached rock bottom and made up my mind to put a stop to the whole thing before it was too late and Brendan's life was ruined forever. I took him round to the house of the foster mother Doris had put me in touch with and asked her if she would look after him for a couple of hours. I then walked back to the flat and took a major overdose. I felt like I had no choice. It wasn't difficult to do. I'd done it dozens of times before. I no longer believed I was going to be able to support Brendan and bring him up as I wanted, but I also knew I wouldn't be able to live without him. I wouldn't have been able to stand seeing him being brought up by someone else. Maybe that was why Mum had to cut all her ties with us once she had walked away, because otherwise the pain would have been too intense. I knew there was no way I would ever have been able to give Brendan up while I was still alive, but I believed he would be better off without me.

As I waited for the tablets to take effect the phone rang. I don't know why I bothered to pick it up at a moment like that, but I did. It was Rodney, the man in the truck, calling to ask me out. I didn't have the nerve to tell him that I'd overdosed, but just hearing his voice through the fog of vodka and tablets gave me a ray of hope and I started to regret what I'd done. The moment he hung up I rang Mum and told her. She made it plain that she was annoyed and disgusted with me but she did at least call an ambulance and the next thing I knew I was back in hospital having my stomach pumped yet again, the doctors ramming the familiar thick rubber pipe down my throat. As I came back to consciousness and the world swam into focus around me I felt a surge of panic. Would they take Brendan away from me now? I couldn't imagine they would allow a little baby to live alone with a mother who was likely to try to kill herself.

But Doris's glowing praises of my mothering skills must have helped. To my surprise the social services were really understanding. They seemed to think it was perfectly understandable that I should be suicidal given my past and all the problems I had. They didn't think it had anything to do with the way I was caring for my baby and they started looking around for more ways they could help me.

I began dating Rodney just before my nineteenth birthday and, believe it or not, on our first date we met Dad in a pub. When I told him that this was my dad, Rodney was all Flash Harry, trying to make a good impression, and they got on like a house on fire. It was only later that I told him about what Dad had done to me, and the way he'd made me go on the game, and Rodney was horrified, telling me I shouldn't have anything to do with him ever again.

From early on in the relationship, Rodney kept insisting that he and I and Brendan should start a life together so he soon moved into my two-bedroom flat with me. I couldn't believe that anybody actually wanted me. Brian was still coming round now and then but his drinking was getting worse and worse and I could see that he was never going to be any help to Brendan, so I didn't protest when Rodney sent him away, claiming Brendan and I were his now.

I really wanted to continue working for David, because the job had given me a bit of self-esteem, but Rodney just wouldn't hear of me working for another man, so finally, after some huge arguments, I had to give in.

Rodney already had three kids from a previous relationship, who came to us at weekends, and I loved the feeling of having a ready-made family – although looking back now I don't know how we all fitted into that flat. It was chaotic and noisy and crowded but it was glorious for me having four kids to look after, plus their Jack Russell as well. There would be no more nights alone in the flat and no more temptations to go out onto the streets to earn money. There was something about Rodney that made me feel safe and I was more than happy to let him take over my life and make my decisions for me.

My most desperate wish was to get social services out of Brendan's life. It was greater than any dreams or hopes I might have had for myself and I knew that we wouldn't need social services any more if I stayed with Rodney. I had no idea what new adventures I was letting myself in for but I started to feel optimistic about the future for probably the first time in my life.

epilogue

When I was in my early thirties, after I had been through years of counselling, Dad came round to see me one day. He had grey hair now and was scruffily dressed in an old red sweater instead of his immaculate suits and ties of old. He seemed to be in a confiding mood, wanting to try to explain why he did the things that he did.

'It was all because your mother had left me,' he said. 'If she'd never left I'd never have touched you.'

His next excuse was that he was always drunk when he abused me, but I knew that wasn't strictly true. While he was in this soul-searching mood he did tell me that he had been regularly raped as a child and he had never told anybody. That may or may not be true, but even if it was, that wasn't any reason to inflict the same fate on me. Telling me the story about himself made him cry.

'Dad,' I said firmly, 'I am not going to be your counsellor.'

I tried to understand why he had done everything he'd done to me, but I didn't think there was anything he could tell me that would make any of it right. Even then he was still angry that I had ever told anyone what went on in private between us. As far as he was concerned I was his property and shouldn't have said anything.

'So,' he said, recovering from his tears. 'If I gave you a thousand pounds now and took you to bed with me and fucked you, that's got nothing to do with anybody apart from us, has it?'

I couldn't believe what I was hearing, or that he thought it was all right to say it.

'Just get out of my house,' I told him.

I knew this conversation was going to be as close as I was ever going to get to an apology from him; that's as far as he could go.

Peter, the man who raped me while Dad held me down, fell into a river while drunk and drowned. I can't claim I felt any sympathy.

Brian fell from his balcony while drunk and ended up with brain damage. I later saw him selling the *Big Issue* in the centre of Norwich. I went over to buy a copy but he obviously had no idea who I was any more.

So many people that I knew have fallen victim to drink and drugs. It takes a lot of courage, luck and hard work to escape from the sort of life I was born into.

In 2006, when I heard about the murder of the five young girls who were working as prostitutes in Ipswich, my heart went out to them. By deciding to walk the streets and have sex with strangers for money they were knowingly putting their lives at risk, but young girls very seldom actually choose to sell themselves in dangerous situations. None of them was born to be a streetwalker. In every case something or someone had happened to them in their childhood to make them think so little of themselves, to make them believe themselves to be so worthless that they were only good for one thing. Such girls have already been turned into victims and are easy prey for any bullies and sadists who choose to go after them, and from time to time for murderers as well.

I could so easily have been murdered. In fact, my father was one of the men who was questioned by the police during that Ipswich investigation because he had a record of working as a pimp in the Norwich area, less than forty miles away from where they were picked up and killed. Girls from Ipswich sometimes used to work on the same block that my mum and I did, the block that Dad introduced us to.

I still have days when I hate him and despise him, and even days when I wish him dead, then on other days I manage to find forgiveness. It's never over and it's never going to be over as long as I live. I loved him very much and I always felt he did really love me in return. I just don't want him in my life ever again.